Parties
Pills
and
Psychosis

Parties, Pills & Psychosis

by Clare Kenyon

CONSCIOUS CARE PUBLISHING PTY LTD

Parties, Pills & Psychosis

Copyright © 2016 by Clare Kenyon. All rights reserved.

First Published 2016 by: Conscious Care Publishing Pty Ltd
33 Crompton Road, Rockingham, WA 6168, Australia
PO Box 776, Rockingham, WA 6968, Australia
Phone: (61+) 1300 814 115   www.consciouscarepublishing.com

First Edition printed September 2016.

Notice of Rights
This book is sold subject to the condition that it shall not, by way of trade or otherwise, be lent, resold, hired out, or otherwise circulated without the publisher's prior consent, in any form of binding or cover, other than that in which it is published, and without a similar condition, including this condition being imposed on the subsequent purchaser. All rights reserved by the publisher. No part of this publication may be reproduced, stored in a retrieval system, or transmitted in any form, or by any means, electronic, digital, mechanical, photocopying, scanning, recorded or otherwise, without the prior written permission of the copyright owner. Requests to the copyright owner should be addressed to Permissions Department, Conscious Care Publishing Pty Ltd, PO Box 776, Rockingham, WA 6968, Australia, Phone: (61+) 1300 814 115 or email: admin@consciouscarepublishing.com

Limits of Liability/Disclaimer of Warranty:
While the publisher and author have used their best efforts in preparing this book, they make no representations or warranties with respect to the accuracy or completeness of the contents of this book and specifically disclaim any implied warranties of merchantability or fitness for a particular purpose. No warranty may be created or extended by sales representatives or written sales materials. The author of this book does not dispense medical advice or prescribe the use of any technique as a form of treatment for physical, emotional, or medical problems without the advice of a physician, either directly or indirectly. The advice and strategies contained herein may not be suitable for your situation. You should consult with a professional where appropriate. The intent of the author is only to offer information for a general nature to help you in your request for a happier life. Neither the publisher nor author shall be liable for any loss of profit or any other commercial damages, including but not limited to special, incidental, consequential, or other damages. The author and the publisher assume no responsibility for your actions.
Conscious Care Publishing publishes in a variety of print and electronic format and by print-on-demand. Some material included with standard print versions of this book may not be included in e-books or in print-on-demand. If this book refers to media such as a CD or DVD that is not included in the version you purchased, you may download this material at www.consciouscarepublishing.com.

National Library of Australia Cataloguing-in-Publication entry:
Author: Kenyon, Clare, 1989-
Parties, Pills & Psychosis / by Clare Kenyon
ISBN 9780994540409 (Paperback), 9780994540416 (Digital)
Kenyon, Charlotte, Cover Illustrator.
Pope, Claudette, Editor.
Kenyon, Adrian, Editor.

Printed by Lightning Source
Typeset & cover design by Conscious Care Publishing Pty Ltd

B/KEN

ISBN: 978-0-9945404-0-9

For My Family

CONTENTS

Acknowledgements
Disclaimer
Prologue

1.	Where Do The Answers Lie?	1
2.	Years 11 and 12	14
3.	Wanderlust	26
4.	The Descent	39
5.	Psychosis: First Time	48
6.	What Mum Saw	59
7.	Finding Me And Falling In Love	72
8.	Sex, Drugs, Breakbeat And Heartbreak	86
9.	2011: A Whirlwind year	106
10.	The Berlin Daze: June 28 - July 2, 2011	120
11.	Berlin And The Clare I've Never Met Before	140
12.	The Hospitals	146
13.	Mum's Story	169
14.	Emerging Through The Darkness	182
15.	Four Years On	195
16	Final Note From Mum	206

Afterword 208
About The Author 210
References 211

ACKNOWLEDGEMENTS

I am indebted to so many people for helping me along this journey………..

Getting the book to the stage it is now would not have been possible without my wonderful editor, Claudette. Thank you for believing in my story, for being the voice of reason, for your encouragement and for keeping me motivated and on track. You have now become a wonderful friend and your continued support means everything. Thankyou to Liz at Conscious Care Publishing for your generosity and for helping me to realise a four-year goal.

In its early days, besides showing my family, I was only brave enough to share the manuscript with two people. Thank you Jess, for taking the time to critique it, all our discussions at the Mill House Bakery are not forgotten; and to Laura for your assessment notes and encouragement. Mosh brought me to tears when she stole the manuscript and had it printed for my birthday in 2013, the first time I saw the finished product in my hands – I will never forget that day. Thank you, Mosh, for your kindness and her support. Thanks to Phillip and Kriste Bridgeman for publishing the original ebook and my Dad who spent hours and hours doing the first edits.

Thank you to everyone who messaged, liked, shared and reviewed the first version when it came out online, and Glynn who championed it without hesitation throughout my time at university. Words cannot say how grateful I am to the people who donated to my gofundme account – without you I would not have got here. To Pip, Beau and Jac for your continuous support and love. To Jason, my partner in life and love, thank you for being there when I wanted to give up, for loving me because of my past and not in spite of it and for always believing in me. I am truly blessed to have three amazing role models in my life — my sisters Charlotte, Natalie and Emma. Thankyou for your advice and love throughout this journey. To my brother Chris and his wife Karissa, thankyou for your support in telling my story and to my brother-in-law and fellow inspiring author, Claudio, for all our insightful discussions along the way. Lastly, to my parents, for never giving up on me, for being so brave and believing in the reasons for sharing our family's struggles. My story is one of hope and recovery because of you, and I will be forever grateful for everything you have both done for me and continue to do.

DISCLAIMER

The following is a memoir of my life, how I got into the drug scene and my subsequent struggle with mental illness. It is a factual account of how I, personally, chose to deal with, and successfully overcome, those events.

It is a chronicle of choices and options that were unique for me and my own set of circumstances. In no way should my story, in whole or in part, be interpreted or construed as an endorsement for drinking alcohol or taking drugs. The opposite is true. I encourage people to stay away from them.

I am not an expert. Any advice given in this book is based on my personal experiences and should not be taken as professional advice. While I am more than happy to talk to people who may be experiencing similar difficulties, seeking professional help should be one's first option.

Other than the names of my family members, all names have been changed to protect people's identities.

PROLOGUE

"If you take drugs again, Clare, you will end up with schizophrenia. It may not happen the first or the second time, but if not, it will definitely be the third."

My body started to tremble with fear; tears filled my eyes and spilled over my cheeks. I buried my face in my hands; what had my world come to?

It was August 2011 and I was sitting in a hospital room talking to a doctor. I had just been to hell and back, arrested and locked up in a psychiatric ward in Berlin after suffering my second psychotic episode. I couldn't believe what I was hearing. I thought schizophrenia was for weirdos and drug addicts ... I was just a fun-loving, music-loving party girl; how could this be my reality?

My thoughts flooded back to all the times I went out to Barrick with Lucy when we went giggling into the bathroom stalls to take our pills. I remembered the feeling of the bass as it thumped in my chest and the adrenalin rush of being in my favourite nightclub, surrounded by people all having a good time. I remembered the shots that we did, the guys that we flirted with, and how much we used to laugh. I thought back to all the music festivals where I'd run amok with Cory, Dylan and the crew. I'd sit on someone's shoulders looking out across the crowd of thousands, pulsing with energy, laughter and love.

How could it have led me here? To a place where those who had been suffering, hurting, craving, had nowhere else to go.

WHERE DO THE ANSWERS LIE?

"What's with this fussing and cussing and fighting, we should be uniting, yet we treat each other like dirt, the world's a jungle, but we're all we got."
World of Hurt – Sub Focus

"Remember the first time you took a hit, remember the feeling, it was the shit."
Joey Seminara, MC Flipside and Danny Nagels – Just The Tip

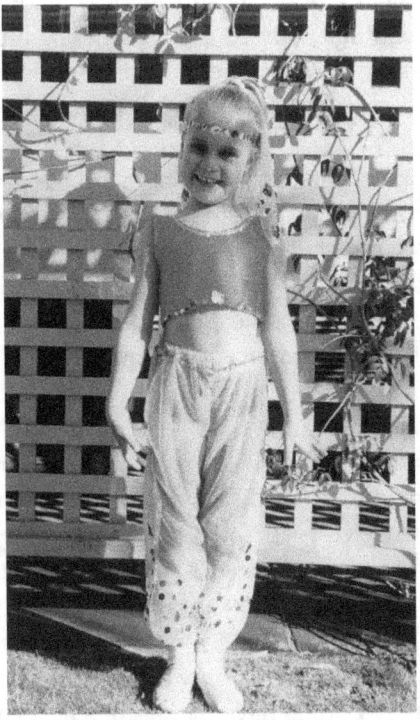

Ballet Concert - 1997

CLARE KENYON

So how far back do you go to find answers about who you are today? Wow, psychologists love to dig into your past, explore your childhood and find reasons for it all. There must be some big, tragic event in your life which led you to taking drugs, but instead why couldn't it just be curiosity, a desire to experience something different or teenage rebellion? I'm not sure anymore. What's that saying Mum would always come up with? ... "Curiosity killed the cat."

I suppose it's all relevant. It's true I was a fairly troubled teenager and when I was in therapy I made a lot of connections as to why I am, the way I am. Although the fighting within my family had started while I was young, I didn't feel so out of place at primary school, as my friends all had their own issues. I went to a lower socio-economic primary school and it seemed, at the time, my family difficulties were quite minor. As young children we spent our days running amok in parks and by the lake, so we never noticed too much. I was quite popular in primary school but when I was awarded a bursary[1] scholarship to attend a private high school, those friends – who went to the local public school - eventually ousted me for wearing a tie and stockings. When I moved to the private school, I was suddenly the small fish in the big ocean and my sense of comfort disappeared.

I was incredibly fortunate to get a bursary, but it was a big change to go into a private Anglican system with so many rules to follow. Mum had always wanted my siblings and I to have a private education as she had been educated at one of the top schools in Perth. Luckily, Cara, my best friend since we were babies, had been at this particular school since Year 6 so I knew at least one other person when I started.

In the beginning our family was reasonably well off. My parents had a great business, publishing magazines and producing theatre and concert programmes. Dad had started this from scratch and ran it successfully for twelve years from a home office. He and Mum had two investment properties, a share portfolio and other investments and had paid off the mortgage on our home.

I grew up in a beautiful, two-storey house, with a large grassed area at the front where we would have cricket matches, and a huge pool at

PARTIES, PILLS & PSYCHOSIS

the back for summer parties. I remember running up and down the stairs of Dad's office, the smell of the clean carpets and the tap-tapping of the computers, thinking how lucky I was to have a father who was this clever. I had a great early childhood, I took ballet lessons, gymnastic lessons, piano lessons and violin lessons, and I played netball, teeball, soccer – my parents tried to give us everything.

But then they decided to expand their business and move into a city office – something that in the end didn't work and resulted in huge financial strain. After months of struggle, the business was put into administration, then liquidated and we lost everything.

Eventually, the house was sold in order to reduce debt. It was a terrible time for the family. I loved our home so much, we all did. I know Mum never got over it and she would occasionally drive past it, just to remember the good times. We had to fight back tears in years since, longing for that simpler life. Longing for times when we used to build cubbies in the living room, skateboard down the hill, have pool parties in our backyard and play hide and seek throughout the many rooms. It seemed like we grew up instantly once our family fell apart, the fun seemed to stop, we forgot how to smile, laugh and play.

When all this happened I was eleven, my brother was thirteen and my sister was nine. Night after night, as Mum and Dad argued and fought, we heard crying, screaming and slamming doors. My sister, Charlotte, and I would huddle together, she was always so frightened. She would cover her eyes and I would cover her ears so she couldn't hear, but that meant I heard and saw everything. I don't know what my brother, Chris, did ... perhaps slunk into his room and turned his death metal music up, but he was all alone.

When my parents separated after their business was liquidated, we lived with Mum, and I didn't see much of Dad as he set about rebuilding his business. I thought maybe it was his way of dealing with a second broken marriage (I have two older half-sisters from Dad's first marriage, Emma and Natalie who live on the East Coast.)

At the time, I saw him as an angry, scary man whom I didn't trust or understand. I felt very abandoned by him but would have done anything for his attention. I didn't know who he was and yet I wanted to know him so badly, I wanted him to love us and come home to us.

Mum was very sick at the time with depression, which I only found out about years later. But she managed to pull us through – I don't know how she did it. As we were now broke, money was a huge worry. But Mum started a mobile dog grooming business which grew out of her love for animals. She worked so hard every day to get me through that high school (and later my sister too) as, even with a scholarship, it was beyond her and Dad's means and I am forever grateful for it.

My relationship with my brother had a profound effect on me, especially during my teenage years. It's hard to talk about it even now because I love him so much and don't want to paint him as the monster I thought he was back then. But I hated him. He was big, scary, loud and aggressive and Mum, Charlotte and I are only little. Chris took Dad's absence really hard. He got into a "bad crowd" at high school; he was expelled from his first school in Year 10 and then asked to leave a second one at the beginning of Year 12. He would be stoned most days at school; he got bad grades, detentions, and was constantly fighting with people. His gang clashed with my old primary school friends who were all at his high school. Those fights were scary, especially when bricks and police were involved.

Chris would scream and yell at us until he was blue in the face and crying. He hated us so much. He had so much pain inside. He would bully me constantly: "You're a fucking loser, Clare, you're a stupid try-hard bitch" … I would hear this over and over again. I hated him saying these things, it made me feel so horrible about myself, and it would echo in my mind day in day out, even when I was at school surrounded by my friends. I didn't know what I had done to him to make him hate me so much. I was scared of him but kept trying to be nice to him or talk to him so he would see I was just his little sister and I was going through the same things as him.

I think the music he listened to – death metal with lyrics about hate and death – contributed to the darkness and pain he was feeling. I

PARTIES, PILLS & PSYCHOSIS

tried listening to it for a while to see if I could understand him more, but after a while I had to turn it off. I felt like it was poisoning my soul.

The three years after he turned eighteen, things really got out of hand ... he would come home drunk most nights and become quite dangerous. I was really frightened of him, and Mum couldn't control his rages. Sometimes we couldn't calm him down. Mum eventually asked him to move out, and he went to live with his girlfriend. Everyone was much happier when he left.

My sister, Charlotte, is my best friend, my spark, my treasure. A beautiful, deep, soulful girl. We have always been best friends; we always wore exactly the same outfits when we were young with our hair in very, very, high ponytails. This changed through our teenage years when we would have ridiculous fights about stealing each other's clothes. Charlotte is one of the most beautiful people I know. She has a presence like no other and a laugh that could make even the saddest person smile. Charlotte is a performer, a singer, and a free spirit who believes in love above all things.

When she was fourteen she developed anorexia nervosa[2]. She was seriously ill for a long time. Those six months were the hardest of our lives. We thought we had lost her, we didn't know how to bring her back, but through courage and determination she fought back and now describes it as the best thing that ever happened to her – and it's true. She would not be the person she is today without going through that hell.

From the age of eleven through to seventeen we moved house every year, and in one year - twice. We would only ever get a year's lease on each property, or the owners would find out about Mum's dog grooming business (and most rental properties won't allow pets). Another time we had to move because we were having so many fights and my brother and his friends would cause issues out on the street late at night, bringing the police around.

Another time we had to move because the ceiling was sinking due to termites. That was the year we moved twice, the second occasion being when we packed up and moved in with Grandma, who lived about 25 minutes from the city on a large property, while we looked for a new place to rent. We were there for about three months before we packed up and moved again.

Most of the houses we lived in were broken down and old, which meant I would always feel embarrassed bringing my wealthy friends over from school, so I usually didn't. The year after high school I actually lived in a tent for three months, in the garden of the house while the shed at the back was being converted into two rooms, one for my brother and one for me.

Having this constant change and instability in our lives meant we never settled down and grew roots. I could never get comfortable anywhere; there wasn't a place I called home, my room, my space. I'm sure my brother and sister felt that way too. But I will give credit to Mum here because it must have been so difficult for her, more than for us, to provide for us all and run a business at the same time when we did nothing but make it worse for her.

Not surprisingly, my first experience with drugs was with my brother. I wanted him to love me, even just like me. So when he asked if I wanted to stay out for a beer with him and his friend, I jumped at the opportunity, eager to connect with him over anything. Cara was over at the time and left with a disapproving look on her face. I think that's when we started to go our separate ways. I was twelve at the time. I had my first beer, first cigarette and first bong[3]. What a night. They showed me how to smoke a bong, and I giggled and floated away, high and happy. It was about 3 am and we were at our primary school. We wandered off to the bakery, taking forever to choose from the range of donuts, cakes and muffins, our stomachs rumbling. I remember giggling uncontrollably because I thought it was hilarious that the baker would know we were high. Afterwards, I felt guilty about Mum because I knew how much she worried about Chris, and I didn't want to lie to her, but I had bonded with my brother and I felt that was the best thing that could have happened.

High school was just too easy, there was always weed around if you

PARTIES, PILLS & PSYCHOSIS

wanted it. Most people in the popular crowd were into smoking weed or at the very least tried it at parties, so it was just a case of who you wanted to hang out with. I was a social butterfly in high school and had many friends, but there were two in particular who really shaped high school for me – a girl named Sophie and a boy named Jack.

I really connected with Sophie because she opened up to me about her family. Through Year 8, I had been desperately trying to find someone who was "like me". Someone who didn't have a seemingly perfect world – wealthy family, happy parents, loving siblings. Sophie fitted the mould, her folks were divorced and she was an unhappy girl, trying to get attention from a Dad who wasn't around.

The night we became friends was just before the start of Year 9. It was Australia Day and Cara and I had been invited to the "popular" girls' party. We were playing drinking games and, after a while I wandered off with Sophie and we started poking around the house. Sophie started looking through the medicine cabinet, grabbed some pills off the shelf, handed me two and swallowed two herself. I shrugged and took them, they seemed harmless. I don't remember the pills doing much to me, but that night has always stuck in my mind – a friendship beginning with risk-taking and a lack of thought about the consequences. It would become our world.

Once she found out I had smoked weed with Chris and his friend, we had another connection. She was starting to get into it too, so we planned a few sessions[4] together. We had a lot of fun in the early days, getting stoned in parks and running amok at school. I would go over to her house most of the time; her Mum didn't seem to care, or was preoccupied with something. So we would have the whole upstairs to ourselves. It constantly smelt of dope, the couches, the walls, and the bed linen. I loved it. I breathed it in, felt calm and would grin to myself mischievously.

We learnt how to make bongs, cannies[5] and roll joints, and had buckets[6] in the bathtub. We dyed our hair black in the bathroom, knowing this would get us into trouble at our strict religious school. Our blonde hair was streaked black so we looked a bit like zebras – we thought it was so cool. Everyone noticed and said something to us. I loved standing out in the crowd. I loved the attention I got when I was with Sophie. We would skip class often and hang out on the oval; we got extra detentions from being naughty while we were sitting in detention and we wrote countless lines. I didn't care, though; I was having fun and I had always had a rebellious streak. These things didn't seem so serious back then, we didn't think we were hurting anyone.

Mum was the only person I worried about, she hated being called by the school. At the time I thought it was just because it took her away from her dogs, but it also looked like I was following in my brother's footsteps, which scared her. I wasn't happy, I was listening to depressing music like Linkin Park, Evanescence and a band called Suicidal Tendencies. Looking back I just needed to talk to someone, but I didn't know how to ask for help, and I didn't think anyone cared.

One day in a science class it escalated when we got silly by sniffing permanent markers, and we stole some matches. Our next class was health education, and as usual we took our time getting there. Sophie had the matches and we were walking across the school through what was known as "the bush court" – a large bush area with several walkways through it. We were laughing and came up with the idea of putting a match in the bin; afterwards we wandered off to class. About 30 seconds later I went back to check if it had gone out and it looked like it had, so I ran back to class. After health education, we went back to our lockers and the bin was no longer there; in its place was a lot of white powder. We looked at each other with wide eyes and burst out laughing.

In assembly, it was announced that someone had almost burnt the school down and the culprits needed to fess up. I sank deep into my seat, with a sheepish grin on my face. By then a lot of people knew it was us. Sophie was dating a guy in Year 12 and had obviously bragged about it. It wasn't long before someone ratted on us. For the next week we ran away from the principal and dean of students. Every time the dean spotted us, he'd bellow, "Sophie, Clare, my office NOW", and we would sprint in the other direction. Eventually we had to go in, and we realised the seriousness of the situation.

PARTIES, PILLS & PSYCHOSIS

I almost lost my bursary, which meant I would have had to leave the school and start all over again somewhere else. The thought of that filled me with despair.

We were suspended for a week, after which we were to meet with the principal, apologise and more or less beg to come back to the school. We did this and were allowed back, but we were placed in different classes. This worked really well – I started going to classes again and my grades went up. Then, because I wasn't spending all my time with Sophie, I started spending more time with Jack.

(Extracts from the diary I have kept since I was 12 appear throughout the book in italics)

Wednesday August 13, 2003

Today was really shit. Yesterday I did something really stupid, I blew up a bin. God knows why, it was incredibly stupid. I think it was just spur of the moment and cause it was fun. Last night my Mum told me that I nearly lost my bursary. I never really knew how bad I was doing at school until last night. But now because I lit a bin on fire I'm afraid it's all gonna start happening again. I'm losing concentration in class again and I find no point to work anymore. I don't want this to happen again, I hate these feelings and I really really don't want to disappoint my Mum as well. She gets a 50% bursary on Char and me next year and if I don't make it worth it she's going to take me out straightaway. I really want to be smart again, I hate being dumb and not knowing the answers and disappointing my Mum, and because I do stupid things I upset Jack as well. All I am feeling now is stupidity. I'm so stupid. I wish things were different. School sucks.

Friday August 15, 2003

So much for trying to get back on top of schoolwork. So much for anything, I'm expelled, it's not definite but I know I am. I'm putting a happy smile on, telling everyone I'm thinking positive but inside

I'm dying. I know the truth. I can't do it. I can't start again. I can't go to another school. Goodbye is too hard to say, especially to Jack. I hate my life, I always seem to fuck it up. Mum's so disappointed in me. I heard her crying all night last night in bed. I hate this so much. I wish I could disappear. I can't be expelled, I just can't or my life will be over. I've lost everyone's respect, including my own. I can't imagine what I would be like without Jack, Bell and all these people. I'm going to miss them like crazy. Goodbye is such a horrible word, I just wish I didn't have to say it to the people I love the most.

Saturday August 16, 2003

I had a really good talk with Bell's Mum today. She actually cared about me. She asked if I was OK and meant it. No one, not even Cara or Jack, when they asked, seemed like they meant it. She was generally worried about me and I found myself telling her things I haven't told anyone before. She said that I had to accept the fact that Dad wasn't there for me anymore and even it he was, and if he gave me a big hug and told me he loved me, was that what I really needed? Is that what I wanted? Would it make everything OK? And I realised no it wasn't. What I needed was something that Dad couldn't give me. I needed to move on without him in my life. So that's what I'm gonna do. Then she asked if I had a good relationship with Mum and I asked myself, do I, because we never seem to talk anymore. Even if we did there would always be a dog interrupting. I've dealt with that, though, because I know she works her ass off to provide for us. But it got me thinking that maybe all this time I had been doing it for attention. Attention from my parents, especially my Dad. But as I've said, I have to accept the fact he is gone from my life. Mrs. Jackson knows I've been experimenting with drugs, alcohol and shoplifting. She said she knew, not because Bellz told her but because she'd been a teenager as well. She asked me if I was lonely and I realised I am incredibly lonely. I'm surrounded by so many people, yet I've never felt so alone in my life. I'm changing the direction of the path I'm taking. I have to stop dwelling in the past of my father and childhood. If I want any kind of future I have to change the way I'm acting and I know that now. I think the damage was done when I started trying before the bin incident but no one appreciated it, Mum didn't seem to be proud of me, I didn't get any praise. I didn't get a hug or anything. I thought even when I do things right I'm not loved or appreciated so I'll just fuck around and then see what happens. Maybe that's what happened; in fact I'm pretty sure it did. But I think I'm back on track now, if only school will give me a second go.

Friday August 22, 2003

Yay School gave me a second chance! I'm not expelled but I have to split up with Soph. But that's fine, I have Jack now and I'm so happy. I haven't seen Jack for two days and I miss him heaps but will see him tomorrow. I'm happy. Genuinely happy. Not even Chris or the fact that I don't have a father for Father's Day on Sunday could make me sad. I'm happy and in love! Real love! Good night!

Saturday September 6, 2003

Dad. Not sure if I have one anymore. It's horrible that he doesn't care. I hate him so much. Father's Day tomorrow. Haven't made plans, he hasn't called me or anything. I miss him but he's not what's going to make my life better. I heard a song last night "my heart will go on", we used to sing it together. Me, my sister and Dad. I just got so sad. I started crying and I never cry in front of people. But it was so overwhelming. Why is life so screwed up!!

Wednesday October 8, 2003

Getting braces next week. Had a fight with Char about Dad. Heaps upset. I hate life. If Jack leaves me now or soon I don't want to be here. Everything is shit at the moment.

Saturday October 11, 2003

I hear the shriek of laughter from my sister as she gets scooped up in Daddy's arms. I remember it was like that for me once. It never is anymore. Maybe it's because I let it be like that. Maybe *it's because I'm scared of him. Some days I hate Dad so much, he comes over only to yell his head off. I remember when it used to be really bad, I remember hearing Chris crying and I remember trying to stand up for Chris only to be yelled at as well. I hate it when my family fights, everyone cries. When my Mum cries I feel like I can't do anything. I just cover my ears but I can't drown out the words that they say – "Fuck you, I hate you so much. I hate my life. This family sucks". When Mum hears this she cries so much. She gets depressed easily because of all the shit that's happened in her life. She tries so hard to make this family work. So hard. I love her so much and all I want is for her to be happy.*

Wednesday October 15, 2003

It's weird. I don't have a father. He doesn't give a shit about Chris or me or Char or Mum. Chris is living with him at the moment, but he pisses off every night so Chris sometimes has to come back here to stay the night. It's weird, I always thought he cared, that I was something in his heart but obviously not. Now I don't want to speak to him ever again. It's like he is dead cause I haven't seen him for so long or spoken to him. It's like he doesn't exist anymore. But what did I do wrong, why doesn't he love me anymore? Where did we stuff up that caused him to stop caring about us? A part of me misses him. He is my Dad, I wish he could just be one for once. I hadn't talked to him for about two months before the other night and he hasn't tried to contact us or anything at all, never comes around to see us. I hate him, he's not my father anymore.

Jack was the second person who shaped my high school years. He was my high school sweetheart, my first love and he'll always have a special place in my heart. He was a best friend, my confidant, and in a way he saved me in high school. Jack was tall, dark and handsome, smart and an obsessed skateboarder. We fell for each other in Year 9, and stayed together until we came home from travelling Europe together four years later, with a brief break somewhere in the middle. We knew each other through and through.

We shared a special bond, and our parents quickly became great friends. I would spend every weekend with Jack, usually skating with

PARTIES, PILLS & PSYCHOSIS

him or watching him skate. He was my entire world, and I was his. At the end of Year 10 after being together more than a year, Jack fell into a depression; he was talking about suicide, and hating the world and its pretentiousness. I didn't know anything about it back then but I tried to help him as much as I could. It affected our relationship because he became very jealous and controlling. He would not let me have any guy friends and we started to fight a lot. We became very upset with each other, so I decided to break it off. Little did I know that I would be a mess without him.

Jack and I smoked weed together, and unfortunately, from my parents, he received a bit of the blame for what happened down the track. I don't believe any of it was his fault – back then we thought it was all so harmless, as did everyone at school. We were all caught up in the days of having compression sessions in caves by the river, jumping off cliffs, late-night parties where we'd steal booze from our parents and sneak off to drink in alleyways or parks... just being rebellious teenagers without a care in the world.

YEARS 11 AND 12

"And I don't want the world to see me, 'cause I don't think that they'd understand"
Iris - Goo Goo Dolls

(Grandma's 80th birthday surprise party, 2005)

PARTIES, PILLS & PSYCHOSIS

The final two years of high school were hard; I began questioning everything and became so lost, so unsure of myself and where I fit in to the world. After breaking up with Jack during the summer before Year 11, I found myself without many close friends. I wasn't a loner or unpopular at school, I just felt as if no one understood me.

I got together with a boy named Liam. He was in the popular crowd, a stoner and also Sophie's ex. I started smoking more weed again – every weekend, then sometimes at night or before school, which meant my girlfriends didn't really want to hang out with me, especially Cara. We hardly talked anymore and I didn't know what was going on in her life. I started hanging out with Sophie again and there were more parties that year where everyone would drink together.

I started to sink away, into my mind, getting sadder as the days wore on, but put on a happy face at school. I became obsessed with the idea of being "free" and went through a hippy phase, listening to Bob Marley, Bob Dylan, John Lennon, Pink Floyd, the Rolling Stones and The Doors, thinking about a world where everyone was at peace. I wore hippy headbands, got my nose pierced and walked around barefooted. I started to notice people more, and became aware of their cattiness, shallowness and pretentiousness.

Because I was with Liam, some other girls invited me to sit with them at lunch, instead of Cara, Rachel, Jessy, Talia and Ana – my group of girlfriends – who I was becoming distant from. I constantly compared myself to these popular girls, as they were in the "in" crowd and very beautiful, funny and clever. I started to get very down about myself, like nobody understood me. I felt like no one liked me, and that I was so different.

So instead of sitting with those girls all the time I formed a close friendship with two guys, Tom and Dean – we called ourselves the Tripod. I preferred to hang out with guys; I stopped comparing myself when I was with Tom and Dean and they would always make me laugh. Tom started going out with Sophie, so Sophie and I became closer still. Sessions started again at her house, with more people, including her neighbours whom I didn't know. But things were different from before.

I felt left out and out of place at her house, plus weed was starting to affect me differently. I didn't laugh as much as I used to when we started together, and it was becoming harder to socialise on it. Sophie was in a bad state, into drugs more than I thought; harder drugs now. She ended up dropping out at the end of Year 11, and I heard that a couple of years ago her Dad made her go into rehab.

I threw a few parties in Year 11; the first one was the after-ball party. I stupidly told a few people at school that Mum would let me have one. Mum was pretty easy going, but it turned out she was very hard to convince. I begged for days and, with a few compromises, she relented.

Liam had asked me to go with him to the Year 11 ball at the start of the year, and we doubled up with Sophie who was then going out with his best friend Nathan. Tom had broken up with Sophie before the ball as she had started to go off the rails and was lying about lots of things, pretending to commit suicide at parties by holding her breath, or cutting her wrists, and just generally doing big attention-seeking things. At the party where she cut her wrists I was so stoned I didn't know what to do and everyone was trying to get me to help her. But she was OK, because the cuts were so small and she didn't lose any blood. I didn't realise how much she needed help, a lot more than me, but no one thought anything of it back then. She was getting counselling at school but I guess it wasn't helping.

The pre-ball was at Liam's house. It was huge, beautiful, grand and regal, so different to my house where the after party would be. I knew everyone there but I wasn't very close to any of the girls. I really felt like I shouldn't have been there but I probably would have felt the same with Cara and the girls over at another pre-party. Even my family stuck out like a sore thumb. My parents put on their best clothes but they were as nothing compared with the expensive labels the other ladies were wearing. As a sixteen-year-old, I was embarrassed that we weren't "like everyone else". It made me feel alone, judged and that I didn't fit into this world at all. I just wanted to run away.

I remember sitting in the limousine with Liam; his two good friends,

PARTIES, PILLS & PSYCHOSIS

Noah and Mitch; and their dates, Mia and Ella, who were the most popular and beautiful girls in our year. I remember feeling very lonely and out of place; the girls were nice and sweet but I couldn't relax around them, I wasn't one of them. Perhaps I was intimidated by all that wealth. I didn't feel good enough for this guy, what with my tiny, broken-down house and family problems. Liam and I weren't really anything by that point, we hardly spoke and he ignored me at school. I was very shy, and he was stoned most days so we just "stayed together" for the ball. We officially broke up after that, but we both knew it had ended ages before.

As well as all that, my grades were very low and I failed a few mid-year exams. I was enjoying some of the subjects, particularly English Literature, and listening to the intellectual discussions but failing miserably. I was shy and timid and never spoke up in class. I particularly enjoyed the poetry analysis and was writing a lot of my own at the time. I was also terrible in physics. Nothing was working out, nothing seemed to make me happy, which just meant I agreed to hang out with Sophie more often.

At home, my brother hated me; he had just turned eighteen and the drinking and the fighting had become more intense. I was so scared of him. The only times he would smile at me or talk to me were when I borrowed his bong or talked to him about drugs. When things got really bad at home I longed to just run to Jack's, to feel safe and protected in his house. But as we had broken up, I didn't have his house to run to anymore.

One night I really freaked out my friends and family. Tahlia, Ana, Cara and I were having a sleepover at Jessy's house and Jessy, as she had always done, started to complain about her life, her brother and money. It was so hard to take when I looked around at her huge house filled with beautiful things and I knew I couldn't stick around to hear it anymore. So I got up and left; about half an hour later they realised I had gone.

It was about 11pm and I just started to walk. I didn't have any place in mind that I was going to, but the more I walked and the more distance I put between me and Jessy's house the better I felt. I walked until dawn, all the way to where Jack lived which was about 20 km away around the river. I was turning things over in my head and trying to make sense of my broken life. I got to the park where I had spent so many happy times with Jack. Then I passed out and slept on the grass. I had been ignoring calls from everyone all night, but eventually I picked one up and said I would be back soon. So I caught the bus back to Jessy's house.

My parents had been going mad with worry, and the girls had waited outside on the driveway most of the night, wrapped in blankets. They had walked around for a while asking people who were out at that time of night if they had seen me. When I arrived at Jessy's, they seemed to me as if they were laughing, as if they thought I had just been out getting stoned. But they were probably laughing from relief. I didn't bother to tell them I had been crying and running away from them, I didn't think they would have understood. And I didn't bother to tell my parents, as I didn't think they would get it either. So I stuck that smile on again and got on with things.

During the walk the only thing that made sense to me was Jack. I started to realise how special he was. I began to miss him very much and regretted breaking up with him. During the Year 11 mid-year holidays, I told him how I felt and of course he wanted me back; he had never wanted to break up in the first place. With him back in my life, I felt better and stronger. I promised myself I would get my grades back up and stop smoking weed. Jack said he would help me with physics too. It worked; by the end of the year I had got my grades up to a B.

Jack's family was amazing, I got along so well with them and they accepted me as part of their family. I went on holiday with them to Bali a couple of times. They invited me to their holiday house down south, where Jack and I would go for long walks on the beach. He would play guitar and sing, and we would smoke weed, cook marshmallows in fires, and stare up at the dazzling stars covering the night sky. These were my happiest memories and where I felt most comfortable. Sandra, Jack's Mum, became a confidante and a mother figure for me as I spent so much time there.

PARTIES, PILLS & PSYCHOSIS

I threw a second party which, after the bin incident, was my other claim to fame from high school. It was the end of Year 11 party. Everyone came, including friends from my part-time job at McDonald's, and there was a heap of gatecrashers. On the day of the party, Jack and I had made weed cookies to sell at school and about ten people bought them. We walked around all day blazed, and it meant everyone was that bit more wasted at the party. My house got trashed, the gatecrashers wouldn't leave, people's phones were stolen and eventually the police came and shut it down. Mum was angry with me for a long time afterwards.

A lot of people in my year were into smoking weed and drinking, mostly the boys though. Our year had a lot of parties, where we trashed our parents' houses, and Jack's parents either didn't know or didn't mind us having sessions at his house. I remember one in particular where we watched the trailer of The Lion King in German and we all rolled around on the floor laughing for what seemed like hours.

While I was lost in my little world in Year 11, throwing dumb parties and getting stoned, my sister started to get sick. I hadn't noticed and I should have been there for her; the guilt from that kills me. Over the summer break before I started Year 12, Mum would say things like: "Is Char OK? She's not really eating much." But I didn't think much of it. It kind of happened quickly; then I realised she was deathly skinny and hadn't smiled in weeks. Mum took her to the doctor, who referred her to a private clinic specialising in anorexia. After that she was admitted to hospital.

Dad had moved back in with us when Charlotte became unwell to create a supportive family environment. My half-sister Emma, who had come from Melbourne to live in Perth to study, also moved in with us. It was nice to move into a bigger home all together, one that resembled our earlier life. It was nice having them around but there was no such thing as family harmony in our world.

I was seventeen at the time and unhappy myself, so seeing my beautiful, bubbly sister – who I thought was so perfect – sink away and hate herself was very hard to bear. She had cut herself up and down her arms, past her elbows – she still has scars now. We would go and see her in hospital and she would smell weird – mostly her breath. I imagined that must have been what the inside of her stomach smelt like – emptiness, hollowness, mustiness. Her nails grew devilishly long and she would click them together, over and over again, and her body would shake. It looked like a mad woman had taken possession of her, and I felt I didn't know her anymore.

To try and escape from all this, I would be at Jack's house as often as I could. But when I was home it hung around like a dark shadow. It became the only thing we'd think and talk about. I used to pretend Charlotte would bounce down the stairs and hang out with me, full of smiles, but she never did. Instead, she was in hospital, rotting away. Our house used to be filled with her beautiful songs; we didn't really notice before because it was so normal, but when it wasn't around it stung, on the inside.

Mum, who blamed herself, bore the brunt of it. A lot of the time they would fight. Mum would get frustrated that Charlotte wouldn't eat anything and so it came down to me to keep the peace. I felt like I should fix her and make everyone OK again. None of us knew the answers, though. I supported Mum as much as I could. Sometimes she would just collapse from crying. Once she was in the bathroom washing her face and I heard this cry of pain and sadness, as if her heart was breaking. I ran in to see her on the floor bawling her eyes out, like she was just giving up. She was sobbing and heaving, like she didn't even have the energy to cry properly. She had no strength left in her to fight these battles. I sat with her, held her and cried with her. I hated seeing my mother like this; it broke my heart a thousand times over and I wished I could have absorbed all her pain. I picked her up and put her to bed. For me this was how I got through it, I wanted to be the strong one for Mum and it gave me a sense of purpose.

There were many nights like this – nights where Mum would fall asleep on the couch with her glasses on, her cheeks wet with tears, and I would pick her up and take her to bed. Mum and I would drive to the hospital every night and then drive home again, sometimes in silence.

PARTIES, PILLS & PSYCHOSIS

Sometimes we would try to piece it all together, try to understand how this once beautiful girl could turn into this shadow of a person, all skin and bones. But there was never an answer. It was one of those things I will never understand, how mental illness works, why it can happen to the very best people.

After about a month, Charlotte had to go on a liquid food drip because she was refusing to eat anything and the doctors said if this continued, she might die. Every time we walked into the hospital, the nurses who got to know us by then would greet us. I knew the path to Charlotte's room off by heart; I remember that feeling when I'd walk in, like someone was punching my heart. I didn't know why my sister wanted to die. I had been depressed myself for the whole year, but I wanted to be there for Mum – I could never see myself leaving her. Sometimes I hated Charlotte, hated her for leaving me, abandoning me, doing this to Mum, being so selfish. And then I hated myself for feeling like that because she was so horribly sick. Guilt used to consume me as I battled with hating her and loving her so much as well.

Friday April 21, 2006

Somehow it's always made out to be my fault. I feel like Mum is blaming me for Charlotte getting sick and because of that I never want to be here. All I ever hear is how sad Charlotte is, how she is not herself anymore, how I shouldn't leave her alone. And then I come home to this sad face that won't talk to me, so I feel even worse. I don't know what to do to make her better. I feel guilty for being at Jack's all the time. The same things come out of Mum's mouth over and over – Charlotte's so depressed, never wants to see her friends. I DON'T KNOW WHAT TO DO EITHER, Mum. Stop making me feel like I have the power to fix her, like I can help her. I can't tell her these things, though – she has enough to deal with herself without worrying about her other daughter. So I tell Jack, but somehow he doesn't know how to cheer me up. Charlie, I wish I could cure your pain, but I can't; it's too hard when I have to deal with yours, Mum's and my own. Sorry.

CLARE KENYON

Friday April 28, 2006

This is messing everything up now. It's even weird with Jack, like conversation is screwed up. I think about everything before I say it. I never used to do that. I feel weird and wrong around him, like I'm doing the wrong things, acting the wrong way. Same around Dad. I feel totally ignored and useless around Mum. I am the lesser daughter. All we're trying to do is cheer Charlotte up and she's so rude, sitting there moping. Sometimes I really hate her. And then she falls into Mum's arms and I'm the devil again. She's so rude; I wish she would snap out of this. She's bringing down everything around her – our first chance as a family in years and she's wrecking it.

Saturday April 29, 2006

Wow, I feel like such a bitch, reading the above. My beautiful sister has gone and I don't know how to bring her back. Now she's lonely and confused in a hospital full of depressed people and I can't make it right. There can't be a God. He/It was invented to make people feel better when things got tough. It was a cop out so they wouldn't have to deal with situations like this. I wasn't around when she needed me most. She was this bright shining star and I hung back in the shadows and I didn't mind – that was who we were. She smiled so big no one could bring her down. But something did. I spoke to Chris about it; he yelled at me when I told him he was being a dick for not seeing Charlotte. "I'm sorry I yelled, Clare," he said, "I love Charlotte, I haven't stopped thinking about her, I've just been really busy, I'm really sorry." They were the kindest words I'd ever heard my brother say.

Friday May 5, 2006

I wasn't there when her life came crashing down because I was so busy worrying about me and the problems in my life. I wasn't there when she needed me; as her sister, I should have known. Now I don't know the right words, I don't know what to do to make it right again. Will she ever come back to us? I don't know this girl; she looks at me with these eyes I haven't seen before. I can't

PARTIES, PILLS & PSYCHOSIS

comfort my mother who is so desperately unhappy and all alone. I don't know what to do.

Wednesday May 10, 2006

We went to the park today to celebrate a friend's birthday. Charlotte looked like a frail old woman you might see in a cartoon. She looked crazy the way she shook and clicked her fingernails together over and over again. She held her hand up, her tiny wrist all floppy, and her head was tilted looking at the floor. She walked pigeon-toed with her shoulders slumped over. She looked mad. This is not my beautiful sister. It won't ever be the same. This weird, crazy girl has taken over.

Eventually, Char came home, which excited and scared me at the same time. I didn't know how to adjust to this new person. But she relapsed straightaway and was admitted to a different hospital. Once she went to this private hospital (one that later I would visit myself), she started to show signs of getting better. She did a course of cognitive behaviour therapy, underwent a lot of counselling and started some art classes where she found a very special talent within herself.

About six months later, she came home, but she was a weak, sad version of the sister I knew. She was "better" though, in the sense that she was agreeing to eat now, but she wasn't strong enough to attend school again. And the thought of school freaked her out anyway. She started attending more art classes and came home with some amazing work. Eventually, she went back to school around the middle of Year 11. I had graduated by then.

A tiny whisper

Lets me know there is life left
Her face shows no emotion
She cannot see through her
Demons of darkness
Who paralyze her every move
She cannot sing anymore
Staring at the ground

CLARE KENYON

I rarely see her sad eyes,
Given up on the world around her
Smaller it becomes
We don't know what will bring her back
Mother weeps for a time when it wasn't so hard
Then weeps again for her guilty wish.
All I can do is hold her
And wish it was me instead of her
Because without saying, the sad whisper
Echoes through the house
We all know it should have been me

I thought my friends at school didn't really get it, but I think now I was just afraid to let anyone in. School was an escape for me, I would paint on a smile and laugh and joke with everyone. Only Jack knew of the nights I cried myself to sleep. By this time I had taken off my hippy headbands, stopped talking about peace and started to wear makeup and my school skirt. I guess I got a major reality kick. I was enjoying Year 12 dance, my elective, where we organised the school dance concert in class together. This was my release, fun and freedom for the year, and I ended up receiving the dance prize at graduation. I felt good about myself -- I was actually good at something and it seemed someone else recognised that too. Dance class and Jack were probably what got me through the final year.

But before I graduated, I got into one last bit of trouble. On our final day of Year 12 a few of us – Sarah, Lucy, Megan, Melissa and Seb – met up early before school and got wasted, taking shots of vodka and drinking UDLs[7] in celebration. A sober friend drove us to school. I went to class but a couple of the others got caught as they paraded around school with a half-empty vodka bottle. So through word of mouth I was caught too and we were all suspended for the rest of the day. The teachers threatened to prevent me sitting my exams but I kicked up enough fuss to stop that happening.

I did well in the exams, and I had Jack to thank for helping me pass physics. The other subjects were never a struggle for me and I was stoked with my results. My mind was elsewhere though – I wasn't

PARTIES, PILLS & PSYCHOSIS

thinking about university like everyone else. Through most of Year 11 and 12 I dreamed about getting away, about exploring another world where there was no pain, crying, musty breath, swearing and fighting. I wanted to get a backpack on and be a wanderer, searching for something but never knowing what it was. I guess I was looking for happiness and peace – somewhere the pain in my chest didn't exist, some place where I was surrounded by people but didn't feel lonely, where people didn't know my past and I could be whoever I wanted to be, where I didn't have the tag of being "sick Charlotte's sister" or "Bad Chris's sister", where I could just be Clare, whoever that was.

WANDERLUST

Capri, Italy - August 2007

"How does it feel, how does it feel, to be on your own, with no direction home, like a rolling stone"
Like a Rolling Stone - Bob Dylan

My parents supported my decision to have a year away before university and Jack wanted to come with me. After graduation our group went down south to the beach for Leavers Week. It was fun, I went to a couple of the raves and partied but I didn't care at that point, I was more or less just rolling with the punches. I wanted to start working and get far away from there. By this time our family had moved again to a property where we got a much longer lease, and my brother had moved out for good. Even though Charlotte was better now, Mum and Dad were still living under the same roof, but were not together. The arrangement was made for financial reasons.

Once home from Leavers, I applied for jobs and starting working at a café and a retail shop. I worked hard at both jobs and was soon offered a manager's position at the shop and full-time hours. I quit the cafe and concentrated on the one job. I enjoyed working there

PARTIES, PILLS & PSYCHOSIS

so much. My boss, Annette, was a gorgeous chubby French woman and one of the other assistants, Maree, was also French and we soon became close friends. The shop was about an hour away by bus and every morning I would put my disk player on and listen to French CDs over and over again, letting the beautiful language wash over me. I thought of nothing other than Europe and felt a sense of peace and calm. I longed to be there so badly. My boss and Maree gave me lessons on most shifts when it wasn't busy and I tried to speak as much of the language as I could. It was so exciting, I was already falling in love with France and I would dream of just staying there and becoming French, and making a whole new life for myself.

I developed a close friendship with Derrick, Annette's husband, who worked at the shop most days. We would talk of travel, music and Europe. After a while I realised I wasn't earning enough, so I got a second job at a pizza shop, where Jack was also working to save up for the trip. Every day after I had closed down and cleaned the shop I raced off to deliver pizzas. Jack and I made a lot of friends working there. Our managers were really cool and we had a lot of fun. I remember delivering pizzas to parties on Friday and Saturday nights ... looking longingly at people having fun and drinking and I would think I was missing out on things. But I was determined to travel, and no matter what I might be missing out on, I knew good things were to come.

Because I had been making new friends, dreaming of backpacking and had completely forgotten about high school, I was actually quite happy. I worked from 7 am to 10 or 11 pm six days a week so I would never be at home, to be reminded of Charlotte, Christopher, Mum and Dad. I spent Sundays sleeping in at Jack's house.

Apart from Jack, I hardly ever saw my school friends. I had become distant from them, I wasn't sure what was going on in their lives and I didn't really care. On the occasions we caught up at parties, I still felt withdrawn and not really a part of anything. My eighteenth birthday party was just another party and once it was over, I knew I wouldn't have to see anyone again for a long time. I was going to Europe on a journey of self-discovery and secretly hoped I would never come back. My sister Emma took me out clubbing once before I left, but I couldn't relax and felt very self-conscious. I left after an hour.

"Sorry," I said to her, "I'll be more fun when I get home from Europe."

I'm not sure why that conversation stuck with me. I guess because of the person I became when I got home.

By May 22, Jack and I had saved up around $10,000 each. It would have to last for six months, so we had a strict budget. I didn't care if it wasn't enough, I was getting out of here. I had lived and breathed the thought of backpacking for almost two years and finally it was happening. I would get my freedom. I threw a goodbye party and to my surprise many people from school came. They gave me presents and cards and said tearful farewells and then they all came to see us off at the airport. I said a sad goodbye to my parents, ignored the guilt I felt about abandoning Mum and got on the plane. I sighed with relief.

The next six months were joyous, hard, eye-opening, fun, strenuous and some of the best days of my life. It was an immense personal journey for me, as well as a journey geographically. We spent the first ten days in England. After some time in London, we went to the north to a village called Hollingworth, near Manchester, to visit my aunt and to see where Dad grew up. Then we travelled to Paris to begin our Busabout adventure, which took us all over France, Spain, Switzerland, Austria, Italy, Greece, The Netherlands, Belgium and Germany. After that, we spent a month travelling by train and bus in the Czech Republic, Slovenia, Hungary and Croatia.

In those six months a lot of significant things happened and every day we wrote travel diaries, as we wanted to remember everything and have the journals for the rest of our lives.

Firstly it was the party aspect; we partied hard. I had been to parties before throughout high school; hell, I threw some of the best ones in school. But I hadn't really done the whole bar/nightclub thing as I was so focused on saving back in Perth. It was exciting and new to me and I loved it. But we were on a fairly strict budget and Jack wasn't the nightclub type.

PARTIES, PILLS & PSYCHOSIS

Wednesday June 13, 2007

After two weeks I'm pretty happy I'm not homesick yet. However, the thought of Geoffrey (my puppy) often pops into my head. Going to these two major cities, Paris and London, that I have constantly thought about, pictured myself in and got excited about, pretty much lived up to my expectations. However, I also found myself a little disappointed. They were smelly and dirty but I guess that having never really spent much time in a big city before, it's normal. I'm not really enjoying the city lifestyle, though, and the mass of tourists. I find myself longing for the coast, the beach and the salty air. Cramped, noisy cities don't suit me – at least I've learned that so far. Jack and I both find ourselves looking forward to our next stops, couldn't really wait to get out of London to see Paris; now can't really wait to get of Paris to see Bern and the views from the rolling Swiss hills.

However, I did enjoy being around French people, their way of life, saying those French words, even if it was just merci and bonjour. The one thing I hate is that we are constantly thinking about money and how much everything costs. I am loving the hostel experience, though, not making too much mess and meeting some lovely people. So yeah the journey so far is going great.

In Madrid we were in our hostel drinking with people we had met along the way. Some of the guys were heading off to a nightclub on the main drag. I wanted to go so badly. I had heard stories of the infamous clubs in Europe, but Jack didn't want to go, and I didn't feel safe going on my own. About a week later, we were in San Sebastian, and again those guys we were travelling with were heading to the club down the road from our hostel. I really wanted to go, but Jack said no ... again. We had a fight over it and I decided to go and meet them anyway. I arrived and one of the girls put a cocktail in my hand with heaps of straws in it; we both took a couple each and skulled, giggling afterwards. After downing another couple, I was having the time of my life. Then Jack appeared and apologised. I was so happy to see him and we had a great night together drinking and dancing. I knew everything was going to be fine.

CLARE KENYON

Friday July 13, 2007

Six weeks, doesn't seem that long but it is. We've been to a lot of places since the beginning. Officially finishing the western side of Europe. I thought I'd feel grown up and become more aware of myself when I'd travel, but if anything I feel younger, smaller. Everyone we meet is at least 21 – I've met only one 18-year-old in six weeks. I still feel like a baby. Everyone on the bus loves Jack, his beard, his hippy ways. Jack knows who he is and people are drawn to that, that's why I love being with him. It sucks to get jealous of him but maybe I'm not, I just feel insecure still. I still have five months to conquer that anyway. So Valencia was great; a day spent on a Spanish beach, what could be better? Madrid was a bit of a disappointment only because we weren't at the Busabout hostel with everyone. We spent most of the night there, though, drinking sangria (I love sangria!), which was awesome fun. San Sebastian was everything I thought it would be after much anxiety figuring out where we were going to sleep because of Pamplona; I'm so happy we get to stay for another two nights. The beaches are amazing, food cheap, friggin' tourists everywhere. I wish we could have seen the running of the bulls, we were only one day away from it! Can't believe it! Bordeaux ... well it was great for the first two days but we were stuck there for four; if we had had to stay for six I would've topped myself! I enjoyed Tours more, there was more life – our hotel was in the centre of town. We took a day trip into a gorgeous old town and explored that.

These past two weeks have been really good. We have eased off on each other, minimised the fighting. I think it is partly because we've been getting better sleep. Actually, I'm proud of us, proud of our creativity and our ability to spend as little as possible. Our best trick is going to the supermarket in the morning and putting a warm pack of cheap beer at the bottom of the freezer underneath the peas so it's cold for pre-drinking later on, and we eat A LOT of pasta. Paying the price of an extra few kilos, though. Jack seems to think it's because of the pill, so I'm going to go off it and see how things go. I'm really excited about the next part of our travels, I hope I just don't get too homesick. Talking to our friends back home, how they are all getting drunk together and having fun just

PARTIES, PILLS & PSYCHOSIS

makes me want to go back. But then a thought occurred, like am I gonna go back to the normal routines just like that, to the high school and party scene and do everything like I had done before; will this experience change me at all? I guess I'll see.

About six weeks later we were in the Greek Islands and things had changed between us. We had started to fight at least daily, just squabbling over little things like money and food. By this time we were about three months into our trip; so three months of being around each other constantly, starting to miss home, and being tired from carrying 20kg bags around was affecting how we treated each other. I was sick of him and pretty sure he was sick of me too. So when the Greek Islands came into view and our tour leader, a young, blonde, bubbly Australian girl, started talking about "how munted" we would all get, I vowed to myself I wouldn't let Jack hold me back.

I got out of my comfort zone, met some girls I got along with and stopped needing Jack by my side all the time. I loved it. I blew my daily budget completely, but I didn't want to let money stop me from having a good time. So I danced with sexy Italian men who were throwing me all around the dance floor, I jumped up and danced on bars, despite the shocked and disgusted look on Jack's face. I skulled flaming drinks and sang at the top of my voice. I danced, chatted and kept drinking until the sun came up. On the mornings afterwards I paid for it dearly; my first seriously bad hangovers were during the two weeks we spent in Greece but it was all so worth it.

Something happened to me on the islands; it was like I was unleashing this inner wild child that I had blocked out. I had locked myself up, hiding myself away from Chris's abuse and Charlotte's sad eyes but in Europe there was nothing remotely close to that and I could let it all go. I felt free and alive, and I realised I was beautiful, I was a fun person and, I loved to party. I had a view of what it was like to be single, making my own decisions, and I liked the look of it. For four years my identity had been connected with Jack, with having a boyfriend. I didn't know who I was without him and I felt it was time I found out. So I sat down with him in Mykonos and told him what was running through my head. I said that when I got home I wanted it to end. I'm not sure if he thought I was serious. However, he said he agreed, as I'm sure he had seen a different side to me that he didn't like, and we were annoying the hell out of each other.

Tuesday July 31, 2007

The past two weeks has had highs and lows. In Venice when I was sitting in my tent dripping with sweat from the 40-degree day I was so low and miserable that all I wanted was my friends, Mum and my puppy. But I put it down to PMS and got over it. Venice is amazing, I love it. So beautiful and I'll never forget the people we met. I love the way the city and the water meet, how different it is to anything we've seen. The people are pretty friendly and San Marco Square, no words can describe it. It was just incredible and especially since for the 30 minutes you are trying to get there all you see are tiny alleyways and waterways, bridges and old buildings and then it opens up to this expansive place. We had our first real gelato there and it was so good. I'm now a big fan of lemon gelato – best out of the five we've tried. So our first experience of Italy was unreal.

St Johan in Tirol in Austria was beautiful but we didn't do anything fancy, just chilled out. Nice cute little town, though, in the middle of nowhere amongst huge mountains. I could not imagine growing up there – so boring. We got to Ancona with heaps of time and nothing to do before our ferry to Greece. The night we spent on the beach with this couple from New York was one of my favourites of the trip. We shared wine and pizza with Anthony and Tasha and had great conversation. We slept on the beach in our sleeping bags. I really felt like a backpacker then, roughing it. The ferry was awful. Loud, hot, windy, screaming German kids everywhere. Nowhere comfy to sleep but we made it to Greece after 48 hours, longest journey of my life.

Thank God we met Justin because Athens was so big and scary at night, we would've got so lost trying to find our hostel. Zeus hostel was a funky place, hated the room, though, but my bed was comfy. We started smoking cigarettes for the first time, it was fun for the first two and then I just felt sick, ha ha. It was a relief to check into a nice hotel with air con and TV and we waited for our Greece tour to start. Jack drank all day and I lay on the bed, napping and

PARTIES, PILLS & PSYCHOSIS

watching TV. We fought a bit. I just get anxious about stuff.

Starting the Busabout island hopper tour – I'm really excited about it. I can't wait to get drunk every night. As time goes on, I notice my age more and more. I feel so much younger and smaller than I did at home which is frustrating because that's what I wanted to escape. There's no way around it. I'm not going to age four years in a week, nor grow 20cm. Sometimes I think we were so crazy to do this at 18. Maybe we should have waited a couple of years, blabla, and it gets me down, thinking maybe it's not as good as it could be. But people are always nice and I don't think anyone but me notices. I shouldn't think so much. I find myself getting so frustrated with Jack at times. I've noticed more differences between us – not necessarily bad, though, just different. I don't think I'll write much more. I'm on the ferry now on my way to Mykonos and all I want to do is free flow.

Thursday August 16, 2007

The Greek Islands – when I think about it, they evoke things like sun, beach, drinking and dancing. And I have had the best two weeks of my life. However, by the end I was pretty sick of the sand, dirt and sleazy boys and most of all the expense. Four nights was perfect for each island and I think I enjoyed Mykonos and Paros the best.

I loved seeing my half-sister Natalie in Santorini – it made me so happy. She is such an amazing person – I hope I can be like her one day. The only thing I regret is not having my girlfriends with me – I know I would have had more fun, and Jack is not a party animal. I am lucky to have friends like Cara, Ana and the rest of the gang. I'm sad to leave knowing we're going back to sightseeing, tourists and intense crowds. I will long for the days in Greece where all we did was lie on a beach and drink cocktails. We've been talking about it so much and we're getting so excited about what's to come.

In about four weeks we are meeting up with Tom and going to places like Amsterdam, Berlin, Prague – places that just seem so surreal to me. I'm pretty buzzed up for it. We are halfway through our Busabout adventure and we have only three months left in

Europe! It feels weird to be counting down, even though it seems not that long at all. In these past two weeks Jack and I have been talking more about the future and us together and becoming more realistic, that we won't be together forever. Now I think we can enjoy the time we have together with more energy and happiness. He's such an awesome person, so playful and fun. I wish this trip would never end and I feel like I am getting a better sense of myself and growing up. I feel happier than I ever have for a long time.

Thursday August 30, 2007

We have explored Italy in the past two weeks and I have really enjoyed it. Something that gives me the biggest buzz is speaking in Italian – just a few words really, Ciao, Bon journo, Preggo, Grazie, Quanta Costa. It's great fun and you get a big smile from the person you're talking to. I really loved Rome, it's a beautiful city and although normally I hate mass crowds of tourists, I didn't really mind; they were also there to discover the wonders of this ancient city. I used to find ancient history boring but wandering through the forum amidst the rubble took my breath away and my mind flooded with thoughts and the realisation that one's lifetime is merely an insignificant timeframe in the history of civilisation. We moved on to Naples. I enjoyed the trek there – it made me feel strong and backpacker-like. My first impression of the city was largely one of disappointment ... the pollution, the stifling heat, graffiti everywhere, the fact that it is the most densely populated city in Europe, and I couldn't stand the air. Thank God for the hostel – air con, kitchen beer, TV and net. It was a relief to finally get a good night's sleep.

I enjoyed our day trips very much. Pompeii fascinated and bewildered me and I tried to imagine what the city would have been like teeming with life down every street. Capri was really beautiful and what a relief to see an island with trees and greenery and gardens. That blue water of the Mediterranean - no sight is better.

Now in Siena, another of the beautiful small towns I love to explore. However, we spent most of the day in between pizza and gelato

PARTIES, PILLS & PSYCHOSIS

shops, although I didn't regret it. It was still laughably culturally Italian and we wandered through the streets anyway. I find myself enjoying this trip more and more. My eyes are beginning to open to the vastness of the world, the culture, the history, and the differences. I love this deeper side of the trip as well as all the partying and I know there is so much more left to explore.

After Greece we were halfway through our trip and Tom came to meet us. We met in Munich and spent ten nights there in a chilled hippy campsite, drinking beer all day with the locals at the beer halls. Our journey together took us up north, to Amsterdam where we got stoned in the cafés, ate a lot of food, saw a sex show and went to a few nightclubs. It was an awesome city and a cool experience but admittedly smoking weed again made me feel very anxious, although at the time I never knew why. It didn't affect Tom and Jack the same way so I thought I was just weird. Our next stop was Berlin and I was so eager to get there. I had studied the First and Second World Wars, the Nazis, and German history in school and found the whole city fascinating. I couldn't wait to be in the place I had heard so much about. I had also been given a "party Europe" book as a going away present and I had read the big section on Berlin clubbing. It all sounded so amazing -- the big warehouses, wacky people, and music I had just started hearing in clubs during our travels.

Unfortunately, being tourists and naïve backpackers, we booked a pub crawl to take us out, it was run by Australians who had no idea of the local underground nightlife scene. It was a Tuesday night as well, but they promised us that clubs were always pumping in Berlin. We got to the club at the end of the crawl and it was virtually empty. My heart sank, I realised then how much I wanted to get out there and live it up. But we had run out of time as we had to catch the bus next day.

I had been thinking about getting a tattoo overseas for a long time, just wasn't sure what. I wanted something that expressed what I felt and one day walking along the Berlin Wall, admiring the East Side gallery I saw a picture and a quote underneath it – "Dancing To Freedom". I felt it embraced the backpacker in me, my desire to be free and on the road, my love of dancing and the power of the written word. One week later in Prague, I had it tattooed in Japanese symbols down my leg. Thankfully Prague also gave me my clubbing fix. We went to a big four-storey club on three of the five nights we were there. We partied on for the rest of our trip, through Croatia and back to Italy. Then we flew to Thailand and Bali for a month before heading home.

Sunday September 30, 2007

We've been away for four months. Wow. It feels unreal, amazing what we've done in this time. Ten days in Munich were the best fun in the world. I fell in love with the city and the German people are the loveliest I've met on the trip, merry and hung up on the simple things in life – food, beer and good times. The haufbrau house will always be one of our happiest memories.

Paris in the autumn was amazing – the beautiful colours and the cool crisp air, the second time seeing the Eiffel Tower was just as good as the first. I loved it.

Now we are in quaint little Bruges in Belgium, and having no expectations, I have fallen in love with this little town and friendly people. Beautiful, winding streets and canals hidden by overhanging trees. Waffles, chocolate and beer ... this country has living perfected! As the days draw on, I feel myself getting a greater sense of the world, people and myself. I am finding a greater sense of peace and happiness than I ever felt at home. When I think about now compared with when we first started, I am amazed by how much I feel like I have grown up and how my confidence has grown. I find myself making conversation easier with people and relaxing into life better. Jack, Tom and I bicker a lot and I'm getting sick of boys and am looking forward to seeing my girlfriends again soon. All in all, I am having such a good time; I don't really want to go home.

Wednesday October 17, 2007

It's been a different two weeks. Definitely fun but not like before. It's great having Tom here but I feel like I'm at home. Nothing's changed about me. Also, I'm feeling extremely tired now, like a weight has come down; maybe it's knowing we're at the end, talk

PARTIES, PILLS & PSYCHOSIS

of university, talk with family. Talk about back THERE.

We haven't been eating well here, though, no fruit or veg and I can feel it now. Maybe we have all become lazy and tired.

As the weeks turned into days before we would be home, this awful feeling started to come over me. I had set out to go to Europe, to find myself, to become happier, to let go, which I had done, but I was away from everything here; it was so easy. Soon I would be going back to everything I hated and was afraid of. I thought returning home meant I had to be that person again – shy, depressed, reserved. I wanted to let go of all that, to dance and party and be happy like everyone else but something kept holding me back. Can I change, would people still accept me? How do I fit back in? Jack didn't like it, what would my family and my friends back home think? I turned everything over and over in my head so much, I was always thinking too much. I didn't know what would be in store for me when I got home, I didn't have a plan, no expectations of anyone, I wasn't even sure if my friends missed me.

Monday November 5, 2007 (15 days left)

How do I feel now? Tired confused, homesick, belittled, picked on. PROUD. It's so hard and weird realising the end is near after so long planning and working, after getting here, flying and landing that first day in London and now soon to fly out. I'm scared about how quick time goes. I'm afraid I haven't changed. I'm afraid to go home in the mess that I was when I came. I'm afraid life will go on the way it once did and I will tumble through it just the same. I'm afraid to go home.

I can see two distinct parts of the trip and I think I enjoyed the first part more. But then again it's so hard to tell. Frustration with the boys has been eating me up over the past couple of weeks. On the second half of the trip with Tom we are lazier, don't explore as much, we eat more McDonald's and don't use the language of the country anymore. That saddens me because Jack and I loved doing it. It just evolved that way really, I don't blame Tom. I appreciate more things now – my youth, my friends, my family. In that sense

CLARE KENYON

I have achieved hugely during this trip. I'm still confused about myself but I have grown up and I know what I like and don't like about people. I want to keep travelling and exploring the world. I love it so much. I want to see all the coasts of the world and write books and stories and editorials about the places I go to and the beauty of the natural world. I want to meet different people and teachers and find real knowledge and awareness out there.

When we arrived home in mid-December 2007, it was to cheers, hugs and signs from my school friends. I was actually a part of something, something I had run away from. These people did actually love me. Did I feel so alone because I just didn't love myself?

I did break up with Jack to our families' amazement but I was ready for something more, to grow up, to continue to find me. I started to hang out with my girlfriends again – I had missed them so much. I had been travelling with boys for six months, doing boy things, sometimes staying in the same clothes for days when it got cold, and now I felt I could be a girl again. We would curl our hair, put on gorgeous dresses, slip on our heels and drink and dance all night long.

That summer was great fun; we were reckless eighteen-year-olds. My friends were amazed at the amount I could drink, the fact that I smoked, I had a ring in my nose and a tattoo, my hair was blonder again and I was bubbly and bright. I had changed, was more confident and a lot more carefree and relaxed - perhaps that's what got me into trouble.

Also, when we got home it became apparent what we had done was an amazing achievement. The people in my life were so impressed and congratulated us. We had spent six months away, at only eighteen when everyone else did the normal thing and went to university. I was stronger and braver than I had thought and these things boosted my confidence.

THE DESCENT

"Now look at this, madness to magnet keeps attracting me, I try to run but see I'm not that fast, I think I'm first but surely finish last... 'Cause day and night, the lonely stoner seems to free his mind at night"
Day and Night – Kid Cudi

When we returned home my school friends were all still hanging out with one another, and no one had formed any new cliques at university. One girl, Maddie, had lost a heap of weight and was really skinny and beautiful. I wanted to know how she had done it and the rumour was something called dexies[8]. I wanted to lose my Europe weight quickly too and made a note to myself to see if I could get them.

At my nineteenth birthday party in February, a friendship began with another girl from high school. Lucy and I were never really close before, just friends of friends and the only time we had really hung out was the last day of Year 12 when we drank together in the morning. She brought two bottles of passion pop to my party and she handed me one as a present, and we chinked and skulled them. Our friendship was born with a mischievous sparkle in our eyes.

My party was also the night when everyone, including Jack, realised I had moved on as I was seen with Nathan, Sophie's ex from school. We had been hooking up for a little while and were sort of together. Lucy was going out with Liam, so it was virtually impossible for Lucy and I to not become friends. Lucy was outrageously gorgeous and had a carefree, rebellious energy I was attracted to.

These two friendships with Lucy and Nathan led me into the world of party drugs. I don't blame either of them for anything that happened later; I willingly took their hands and followed them into it. I was also the one who made the decision to continue on with it, no one told me or pressured me to do it. I was curious, I wanted to party and I liked these people, plus life in Perth was pretty boring compared with Europe. At the time I had little direction, and I am the first to admit I was impressionable and easily influenced. I also wanted to feel a part of Lucy, Liam's and Nathan's group; it seemed like they were having a lot of fun together and I wanted to join in on it, especially after the miserable time I had in Year 11.

Anyone who's ever tried ecstasy[9] will probably remember their first time. My first time was over that summer at my second music festival. Another girl from high school, Holly, had a hook-up that we trusted. At pre-drinks we decided to get on it together at the festival – Cory, Tom, Lucy, Holly and I. It would be the first time for all of us except Lucy. We were also going to meet up with Liam and Nathan and some other guys from school who were also planning to take pills.

Lucy kept saying – "you will feel it, you will feel it." And it was an impatient wait, maybe 30 minutes. It came only slowly, but once it was there, Lucy was right – you knew. I suddenly wanted to touch things and feel things. I looked at Lucy and Cory across from me and wanted to hug them and tell them how much I loved them. Nathan was holding me and it felt so good. He was running his hands up and down me, tickling my stomach as I stood in front of him watching the DJ. I couldn't stop grinning, and everyone around me was smiling too. Everyone was happy, everyone was feeling what I was feeling, and we were all sharing the moment.

I had transcended to a different world where only euphoria existed and all I cared about was this moment in time. A feeling of giddiness and energy coursed through my veins. My body had taken on a whole new element of being. I was taking in deep breaths and I danced and danced and danced. And talked and talked and talked. And danced and talked and danced and talked. I felt warm inside and outside, Nathan and Lucy kept handing me water bottles to have a sip of. The crew was taking care of us first-timers. We danced and listened to artists like Eddie Halliwell, Sven Vath and John Digweed, artists I was beginning to recognise, music I was learning to love.

We were still high when the final act – The Chemical Brothers –– started. The lights, lasers, sounds and colours were so mesmerising. The visuals they had set up were one of the craziest things I had ever seen. I remember we all tried to jump up and grab the lasers as they flickered over the crowd during the set. At one point I just closed my eyes and tried to savour the feeling, the memory, the sound of the crowd raving.

Soon enough, we were heading to the beach as the boys wanted to have a session. Everyone had a bong, one girl and I said no but I felt a bit awkward about it, that perhaps I should have had one just to be a part of the group, and I told myself I would next time. Lucy was having bong after bong after bong, almost like it was a baby's bottle. I laughed my ass off when I saw her bloodshot eyes and Liam was just shaking his head grinning. Nathan and I eventually left the group, we fooled around in his car for a while and then he dropped me home.

After that I hung out with Lucy, Nathan, Liam and the guys from high school more often. I would go to drum n bass gigs with them and that's really where my love for dance music started.

Have you ever experienced something that made you so happy you could never forget it? That is what my first drum n bass experience was. It felt like it was something I had been searching for my whole life – something you knew was just right for you. It was energetic and crazy and euphoria rushed over me as I listened to the DJ, even when I wasn't high on ecstasy. It blew my mind. I watched the ravers to start off with; I watched how when the bass dropped everyone would lose their shit on the dance floor. Minutes later I was involved too.

But as the days and weeks wore on, partying and taking drugs started to heavily affect me. At first I thought it was just side-effects from regular use and it was the same for the others as well. I thought they just hid it really well, plus they had fairly cruisy jobs to go to, whereas university was tough to keep up with. I was studying history, politics, French and psychology at university but was getting very far behind in all units. Instead of writing up assignments I would be partying, recovering or getting stoned with Lucy or Nathan.

Things changed when Dad took me to a wealth creation seminar. It was an incredible day and I really enjoyed myself. I listened to millionaires telling their stories and they made you believe you could be just like them. It was very effective marketing, especially to a nineteen-year-old who didn't know much about the world.

They said things like: "If you do this, you WILL find your freedom. Think if you could do exactly what you want every day, what would it be? You can do this."

For me, that was travelling. I still wanted to get out of Perth again so badly. Even though I was partying and having fun, I wanted to get away from reminders of my sick sister, my horrible brother and my unhappy parents. I guess partying was that kind of escape, but I knew it wouldn't last forever. Plus I still had that overwhelming sense of guilt about my family, that it was all my fault and I wanted to fix it and make them all happy. Money seemed like it was the answer. It was also an easy escape from university since I was failing.

So when the day was over, I said to Dad: "I can do this, I can start up an internet marketing business and make us all rich", and in the back of my mind I was thinking "and get me out of here again".

After a small discussion my family was on board and I dropped out of university that week. I remember smiling to myself when I arrived to withdraw. I felt like we had found a secret no one else knew.

"Sucked in, I'm going to be rich and travel the world while you all slave away at university," I thought. I was attracted to the lifestyle they were promising at the seminar, the music they played, the energy of the room, the excitement in their voices and the goals they asked

PARTIES, PILLS & PSYCHOSIS

you to write down and set in your mind. It was powerful and as my psychotic symptoms had begun to develop, I thought it was "meant" for me.

Wednesday April 2, 2008

Out of control. Actions and reactions. Consequences.

I feel anxious. I can't shut my mind off. Everything keeps turning over and over. My friends – I have them right? I wish I could stay in my PJs forever and give up. But I'm a fighter, that's what they say anyway. I'm always the shoulder to cry on, the one with the advice.

I came home and it was all about me, but I took it too far. I crashed and burned. I'm not strong. I'm just scared shitless and pathetic because I copped out. I bailed. Try hard. In the shadow of a brother's reputation. In the shadow of a beautiful sister. I can't remember things, I'm confused about so many things, I feel like I'm not in control of my mind. I feel sick, so sick. I've let people down and made bad decisions and I can't numb it anymore. The past keeps catching up with me and I can't block it out.

No one to turn to, nowhere to run.

Europe. What changed, what happened? Why have I forgotten everything? So hard to put everything in order.

While I was setting up my internet marketing business, I also did an online course learning how to trade options, foreign exchange and commodities, which I really enjoyed. I got a job at the local IGA with Tom and started working again one day a week with Derrick, my old boss at the job I had had before Europe. So I had a fair amount of money coming in, but being nineteen, I spent it on partying.

Being out of the study structure, meant my mind could float off a lot. At the IGA there were young people who took recreational drugs and I got along with them, so when Nathan and I broke up I still wasn't away from the drug scene. In fact, I made more friends within it by being out a lot. It had started to get a bit awkward with Nathan, perhaps because I was becoming sick. We never spent any time together and he worked away a lot. We stopped talking after a while and officially ended it via a text message.

I developed a close friendship with Derrick; he became a confidant and a huge supporter of my business goals. We started going to the gym together as he was training for a fun run and I was keeping fit. He would also drive me to work on the days of my shift. He would laugh at the "new Clarey", the "party Clarey", as we both remembered how shy I had been before I left for Europe. I opened up to him and told him how I felt when I thought I found a happier version of me in Greece. Derrick didn't mind me smoking weed and I took full advantage of that. I would rock up to work stoned most of the time and he would laugh at it – sometimes he would buy me munchies[10]. But it was a bad thing, having an adult whom I looked up to endorsing it. I also trusted him, so when he hit on me I felt disgusted with myself, used and sick. I hadn't realised that smoking this much weed had affected my judgement and decision-making skills, my mental state in general.

Saturday April 5, 2008

Tonight I tried to make a CD so my friends would like me again. Nowhere do I fit in. Not with Cara and Ana, not with Sarah and Lucy, not with Nathan. I'm so scared to take my own journey. I wish I could take up and leave, but I feel so different and something is holding me back. I can't relax around my friends or feel good about becoming one of the crowd at university. Nothing is right. Is this real, though, or am I just depressively drunk? What's going on? Life's so hard and unexpected. I feel sick, not stomach sick, but mind and body. Maybe I should see that counsellor, Victoria, again.

Wednesday May 21, 2008

The worst night of my life last night. Chris came home about 1am screaming, crying, yelling for Dad again. He came in through the gate, slammed it hard and broke it. He was so drunk and could not stop swearing. He started to yell at me when I came out of my room scared. I tried to get him to calm down. He screamed at me "fuck off bitch" over and over again.

PARTIES, PILLS & PSYCHOSIS

Mum came out to try and calm him down and he wrestled with her. I was so scared he was going hit her. Mum wrestled him to the ground and he was still screaming, "Where is Dad?"

His girlfriend Karissa was there too, crying, trying to talk to him, to get him out of this horrible world his mind was in. I sat on his legs, Karissa held his arms, Mum sat on his stomach and slapped him over and over again.

"Are you going to hit your own mother, are you? Are you going to hit your own mother?" she repeated. She started crying. I looked up at the stars and thought of Paros floating topless in the water, Prague dancing in the nightclub, San Sebastian staring out at the Atlantic Ocean ... freedom. Why did I come home, why did I come back to this?

After what seemed like an hour he calmed down, tears still rolling down his face. I wanted to hold him so badly, tell him, "I know, Chris, I feel it too". I wanted to make him feel better; my big brother was in so much pain. When he calmed down, he got up and Karissa and he went off to bed. Mum was crying and I held her, told her it would be OK. She was shaking terribly. "Fuck your father," she said.

Monday June 2, 2008

An after-thought
Tiredness so consuming
Unhappiness so far-reaching
It's so hard to say and feel this
Am I allowed to?
I don't want to fail my parents
There's so much more I want to say but don't know how

I'm the strong one, the capable one
I do not fail
I'm not sure if I can be unhappy, if I can break down
Am I entitled to?
I wish I could hurt myself so I can show how much my heart hurts
I'm so tired of feeling this way

CLARE KENYON

I'm so tired of doing stupid things to mask my fear

Friday June 20, 2008

Again it's this disjointed feeling I have and I can't stop thinking about Europe.

How, from being so high, can I come down so low?

I remember those last weeks in Asia, I was anxious to go home, so unaware of who I was but I had the greatest summer ever where I forgot everything about my family, had fun with my friends, let myself have fun. Drunk almost every night. But it started to feel so hollow, I couldn't shut out that deep part of my mind ... now I'm just as lost as before, so unaware of myself, no matter how hard I try to block it out, trying to adapt myself in all different ways. I don't pretend around Tom or Jack, though. They know, I think. I'm so confused and I have no one to reach out to.

I want to leave again so badly. I don't know if I have it in me, I'm so chicken shit, but I wish I could just step off the plane in London and get lost in the crowd of millions and then figure it all out later.

Wednesday July 2, 2008

How did I end up like this? This isn't me, is it? Where has everything I learned and experienced gone? WHO AM I?

Confusion. Getting so wasted, that feeling of not caring, letting everything that's bad and crap wash all over me and kissing someone who doesn't care either. Is that my life?

I feel my friends slipping away from me. I'm not a nice person anymore. I am so concerned with myself, how I look – I never used to. Or did I? I have fun, don't I? I feel like shit now. I feel so weird every Monday after a big weekend now, I feel like everything I did was wrong. It's not so much the hangovers, I can handle feeling sick, but it's the guilt, the regret hangover I hate. I can see the looks, I remember those eyes, people who knew me, looking down, the "you've changed" look.

PARTIES, PILLS & PSYCHOSIS

I want to go off by myself again. I don't want a big send-off, just me quietly slinking away so no one notices.

I had lost contact with most of my girlfriends from high school, especially Cara, who had gone down a different track towards Christianity. I know they were really worried about me partying so much, but after a while they stopped saying so because I would get defensive and wasn't able to see what they saw.

One of my best friends from school, Sarah, called me one day and yelled at me for 45 minutes to stop smoking weed because I was getting paranoid. She could see it. She could see how I was acting around my friends, awkward, not being able to get out of my head or relax.

She told me to start looking after my sister who was getting sick again. I had walked in on Charlotte cutting her wrists again. I didn't know what to do and what with Derrick, my sister and my building paranoia, everything came crashing down one weekend.

PSYCHOSIS - FIRST TIME

"I know just what it feels like to have a voice in the back of my head, like a face that I hold inside, a face that awakes when I close my eyes, a face that watches every time I lie, a face that laughs every time I fall."
Linkin Park – Papercut

A painting from the hospital - September 2008

It started months before I ended up in hospital. I look back and can pinpoint a change in my mental health – it was when I started smoking more weed, taking ecstasy and dexies. I became on edge about everything and very anxious. I over-analysed everything, turned things over, hardly slept at night, had that eerie feeling someone was watching me constantly. I couldn't make decisions for the life of me, I stressed over little decisions that have no consequence, everything became a bigger deal than it should have, like having soup or a sandwich for lunch and what having it "meant". I was constantly scattered and I couldn't make normal conversation with people anymore. I started to think all my friends hated me and people were laughing behind my back.

But I didn't think anything of it because I couldn't explain it, and

PARTIES, PILLS & PSYCHOSIS

it was a gradual build-up of symptoms. I thought I was more or less normal and the thoughts I was having were true and real, until nurses explained that sick people are the last people to realise they are sick. We would all drink heavily at pre-parties so it calmed the anxiety I felt, and I spent every weekend in nightclubs where I felt most comfortable. I had always been a survivor too, I never fessed up when I had problems or felt upset. I didn't feel there was anyone to reach out to about it because I felt so weird and confused; I didn't think anyone would understand. It was like I was two people, normal on the outside, laughing, joking, taking drugs, but on the inside I was consumed with fear and it was a part of everything I did, said and thought.

One weekend I went on a bender. It started on the Thursday when I went out with my workmates. We started drinking at work, pouring cruisers into bottles so the management wouldn't know, and we stayed out at a club till the early hours. On Friday after work I went out to a gig with Lucy. On Saturday night our crew got together and had drinks at a pub, then we went out clubbing in Fremantle. I should have noticed something was wrong that night. I had forgotten my ID and rang Dad to ask him if he would drop it off. I told him it was in my little black bag but didn't realise I had left a baggie[11] of weed in there. So of course, Dad saw it while he was searching for the ID and went crazy at me.

That night was a mess, it was a struggle to make conversation with people and I couldn't concentrate on anything. Towards the end of the night, everyone had left but I stayed dancing with a guy I had met. I guess I never wanted to come down from the high. I had a few dexies and was quite drunk. Eventually I got home OK and I drifted off to sleep with the sound of teasing laughter in my ears.

The next day I went to the Conscious Living Expo in Claremont with Mum and Dad and Emma. My thought processes were so strange, but at the time I believed my delusions were real. I thought the whole event was about and for me. I interpreted the usual glances people make when a new person walks into the room as them thinking, "Here she is, here is the amazing Clare".

People were looking at me differently and I thought it was because

CLARE KENYON

I was famous, but I didn't know what for. However, they were taking me on a journey to find out. I walked around with Dad and I remember laughing to myself because everyone knew who I was, I was famous! I must have looked crazy, walking along laughing to myself, nodding at people. On the train home I heard a guy on the phone organising a party or a Sunday session, and I knew he was organising it for me and the whole of Perth was coming for one big crazy party in honour of me.

When night fell and I clearly wasn't at a party, I stayed in my room out the back. I had a cone[12] and went on the computer listening to music. I started to think I was on a journey again and began clicking link after link after link, thinking it was taking me somewhere. I was up all night, getting more and more confused, thinking I was getting messages from cyberspace, telling me things and if I just kept going I would find out what it was.

Eventually the sun rose. I avoided Mum inside the house, stuck to my routine and went to the gym. When I got there, again I felt like everyone knew me and could read my thoughts. It made me believe I was on some special quest. Watching the TV while walking on the treadmill, I started to interpret the news feed as being about me, but it was becoming negative, like they were warning me about something. I started to get scared and even more confused and tried to get home. But I realised I had lost my keys somewhere. I couldn't find them, nor did I have any money for the bus. I left my car at the gym and I got on the bus, mumbling something about no money and I could see the pity in the bus driver's eyes. I looked homeless.

When I got home I freaked out even more because I realised I should have been at work an hour ago. Mum was home and started yelling at me: "Where is your car, what is wrong with you?"

I couldn't answer, I couldn't get any words out or form any rational thoughts. I tried to speak what was in my mind but as soon as I did I realised how insane the words sounded. So all that came out was a little giggle, which really freaked Mum out. I thought she "knew" about it all anyway, so I didn't really need to explain; I thought she was just "testing" me. I hadn't eaten anything for two days which affected

PARTIES, PILLS & PSYCHOSIS

my brain power and the ability to function properly. Mum started looking through my room, found my bong and went crazy. She knew something was up. I was acting so strangely so she took me to the doctor's.

I tried to explain myself to the doctor but he didn't get me. No one understood I was getting messages, important messages, and it was imperative I figure out what for. I managed to convince the doctor I was OK, so he just thought I was suffering from withdrawal.

Monday September 8, 2008

Dr. **********

Mum says delusional, incoherent rambling, messages from radio and computer. Lost car this morning got lost at the gym, unable to complete a sentence. Seeing insects crawling. She sees her as unraveling from the beginning of this year. Stopped university, not looking after self, wanting to go out partying, clubbing, drinking too much, smoking weed. Then spends days dissecting the event and worried that friends do not like her, should have said this or should have said that etc. etc. Very worried about what friends think.

Clare says that she is a normal teenager who is just hungry and tired. No sleep last night. Discussion with Clare – getting messages through Triple J radio station when driving here this afternoon. Last night up all night on computer, on Facebook, getting really confused. Thinks they are making fun of her. She says she realises this is not normal and wants it to go back to normal. Says she thinks her friends may be warning her to stop using it so much. Lucy had a bad experience and stuff.

Uses heavy amount of marijuana on the weekends. Says she loves her week, chills her out. Last used on Wednesday – says nil last weekend. Says not seeing anything weird. Avoids eye contact. Has also been using ecstasy and dexies. Doesn't inject anything.

Examination:

CLARE KENYON

General:

Speaking quietly. Some speech mumbled, though most discernible. Some confused. Often perplexed expression. Looks tired. Occasional smile and laugh.

***Weight:** 48.5kg*

***Blood pressure (sitting):** 110/70*

***Pulse (sitting):** 84*

Diagnosis:

Likely drug-induced psychosis.

Actions:

Prescription added: VALIUM TABLET 5mg 1-2 prn for insomnia. And see tomorrow.

He then signed me a certificate for work and we were on our way, Mum looking relieved. She gave me some Valium and expected I would go to sleep. But that night I stayed up on the computer again, clicking link after link after link. Mum told me afterwards I had about 40 web pages up. It's hard to explain the feeling; it was like a heaviness surrounded my head as I went deeper and deeper into the delusion. I was listening to music in my room on my laptop. I was convinced someone was watching me from the garden and whenever I went into the main part of the house that person would come into my room and change the song – giving me some sort of "message".

At first I thought it was funny. I even went outside to try and speak to the person. Then I became scared. Part-way through the night I must have woken up Mum as the next thing I remember was being in the emergency ward of a hospital. I have blocked most of it out. Mum had to tell me what happened. Even today, I still try to piece it together. I remember being very scared and angry and wrestling with Mum over the computer, and later being in a dark room screaming when a doctor tried to give me a needle. I remember trying to run away a few times, Mum chasing me and dragging me back into the hospital.

PARTIES, PILLS & PSYCHOSIS

Tuesday September 9, 2008

The assessing psych team member

Alma Street Psychiatric Assessment Service
Alma Street
Fremantle
Fax to: ********

Dear *****

Re: Miss Clare Kenyon DOB: February 17, 1989

Thank you for seeing this female aged nineteen whom I saw yesterday. I think she has a drug-induced psychosis. She was mildly delusional and quite perplexed yesterday, likely due to drug effect/withdrawal from heavy cannabis use in combination with other recreational drugs (alcohol, ecstasy, and dexamphetamine). It seems that despite the use of Valium overnight she has become more delusional and erratic, with her mother reporting significant visual hallucinations. This is her first presentation with psychotic behaviour, and not surprisingly it is causing severe anxiety to her parents. Clare is also quite distressed today according to a phone call I have just received from Serena, her mother. I would therefore be most grateful if you could urgently assess and advise today. I reprint the notes that I made at consultation. As requested, they will be turning up at 4pm today.

Sincerely, Dr ******

I guess I could describe this episode as like being in a tornado – thoughts whirling around me, everything loud, in utter confusion and panic. Then when it stopped, falling back down to earth, looking around and seeing everything was different, reality had shifted; things broken, ruined and twisted. It was as if something had suddenly switched in my brain ... from being high and happy to somehow interpreting everything in an intensely paranoid world.

It would start when someone, even my best friend, or Mum, would say something to me, and I would think they were teasing me or laughing about me and I couldn't just brush it off. I would think everything in my world was "connected", people knew what I was writing in text messages and emails and on Facebook, and it was all the same thing, infused together. Everything people said had an ulterior meaning.

My world quickened up when it happened, everything around me became faster. People's conversations would go quicker, so I missed half of what they were saying and therefore didn't understand they were not talking about me. I would just catch bits and internalise everything – things I would read in books, newspapers, on walls were about me. I couldn't control or talk myself out of this state. I couldn't form any normal, sensible thoughts. I was far from what was real.

Anxiety would seep through me. I could feel it rising from my toes coursing through my body. It was so overwhelming sometimes, I couldn't even move to go to the toilet.

I had no idea what was going on when it happened, and it happened a few times before I ended up at Alma Street. I was sinking further and further into this paranoid world where street signs meant something different to me, where TV reporters would stare directly into my eyes and accuse me of being a chicken. Custom number plates meant something, t-shirts with writing on them were a code meant for my eyes only. When an ambulance was driving in front of me I would just freak out, thinking I was doing something wrong or something bad was about to happen. I constantly felt like someone was watching me.

Everything had a message or was a code for something. I couldn't go to sleep because I was getting so close to finding out what it all meant. I listened to Tom and Alex on Triple J for about fifteen minutes, my eyes wide and scared, and I heard them laughing about me for all of Australia to hear. Everyone knew my thoughts and they were all laughing at me.

Then the next day I woke up in a hospital ward. The room I was in smelt weird, I could hear people yelling and trays clinking. I looked around in a bit of a daze. I was still wearing clothes from the previous day, and then I realised this was not my bedroom. The events of the

PARTIES, PILLS & PSYCHOSIS

previous night came flooding back and I almost lost my balance. I felt very scared again but I walked out and saw some people smoking and went over to them.

"Hey," said a lady with two teeth missing.

"Hey," I mumbled back.

A cute boy offered me his pouch. "You roll?" he asked.

I didn't but I fumbled my way through it. Then he started speaking really quickly and urgently.

"Just do it," he said, as he stared intently into my eyes.

"What the fuck! Do what, do what?" I thought. I hadn't left my paranoid world just yet.

I took a drag and that's when Mum walked in. When she saw me smoking, she started yelling at me, and she handed me sanitary pads in front of everyone. People around me sniggered and I just wanted to die. I followed Mum back into the dining area, thoroughly pissed off.

A doctor came to see me. He was an older man, with a nice smile. I couldn't look him in the eye. He asked me questions over and over again about my drug use. I didn't know if I should tell him. I thought I would get into trouble and I didn't want to get Lucy into trouble. Eventually, he told me he already knew, because they had taken blood samples the night before. He said I had dexamphetamine (dah), marijuana (I always laughed how adults said marijuana instead of dope or weed and reallllyyy pronounced it) and ecstasy.

He ordered more tests and I was sent away when I wouldn't talk to him. I didn't trust him; he was laughing at me behind my back.

The first week was really hard ... wrapping my head around where I was, talking to other patients and basically just accepting what had happened to me. Days would consist of group therapy, art classes, cooking and making bracelets. I made a few paintings, which I liked, but it made me feel like I was back in primary school.

I still didn't know how to, or want to, communicate with my doctor and nurses, so Mum relayed everything for me. Every day she told them what I told her and she explained what happened that weekend before I was admitted to emergency.

I heard her say: "I saw a gradual deterioration in Clare over the past couple of months after she got home."

One day the nurses handed me a sheet of paper. Psychotic Episode and Psychosis – Symptoms and Treatments, it read.

It told me psychosis was an illness causing people to misinterpret or confuse what was going on around them. Such as hearing and seeing things that are not real, or delusions where something was strongly believed to be real but was not true. It said the way a car was parked outside a house could mean to someone with psychosis that police were watching them. As I read on, the sheet also described confused thinking, where everyday thoughts could become muddled making sentences clear or hard to understand. It told me the illness was making me have difficulty concentrating, following a conversation or remembering things. It told me my thoughts would speed up and my feelings and behaviour could change quickly without an apparent cause. Psychosis was often frightening for the person and misunderstood by others and it usually happened in adolescence or early adult years. With treatment, most people made a full recovery and the cause was probably a combination of genes, drugs and stress.

It was like reading about the past couple of months of my life. Everything finally made sense ... the thoughts and feelings I was having, but above all it explained my paranoia and thought disorder.

Over and over again, the doctors and nurses would say to me: "You can never do drugs again." At first I almost laughed at them – they couldn't be serious, it was too much fun and I wasn't going to be the one left out of it, but I eventually let it sink in. When the doctor

PARTIES, PILLS & PSYCHOSIS

told me I had psychosis, it was like a weight had been lifted from my shoulders. So I really was sick, it wasn't just me, it was an illness many other people suffered from ... what a relief that was to hear.

I underwent a lot of counselling in hospital, and the nurses really took an interest in me. Once I had regained contact with reality and was able to speak my mind properly, the nurses – particularly one called Rex – talked me through my life.

I had never had to sit down and think about my childhood. I had blocked most of it out or run away from it to Europe. Rex made me recognise things in my past had affected me greatly and he made me come to terms with them and accept them. He made me realise I was trying to fit in with a group from high school I was never really friends with in the first place, and I cared too much about Nathan who didn't for a moment think about me.

Finally, I was able to talk to my parents about the real reasons I had left for Europe; how Chris's bullying and Charlotte's illness had affected me; how I felt left out of the family, not needed or wanted. Now I had addressed these issues I felt so much stronger. It seemed all I needed all this time was just to get it all out, talk to someone, and stop bottling things up.

In hospital, I met a boy called Mark. We became close as we both had the same illness and he was about my age. Sadly, though, he said he had psychosis due to stress and lack of sleep, whereas for me it was drug-induced and all I had to do was not take them anymore. It took me a while to understand it though, I thought it was a big joke at first, particularly when Mark asked me what was wrong and I answered: "Oh, I just analyse everything."

He said: "What's wrong with that?"

I said: "I know, I shouldn't be here."

He looked at me strangely after that.

Now I know it showed I didn't really understand my illness and still didn't believe I was actually sick or didn't want to believe I was sick because that meant I had to give up partying. In a teenage rebellion way, now that someone told me I couldn't do it, I just wanted to do it more.

The other person I hung out with in hospital was Jacob, a boy who seemed familiar to me but I was never certain if I had met him before. He was really cute, blonde with blue eyes. He said he had been locked in there three times, all because of weed. On his nineteenth birthday he was locked in an empty room kicking, screaming and yelling at the walls but he had to be in there because he had tried to hurt his mother, and it was voices in his head had made him do it. It was weird to hear this side of weed. Growing up, we had all just had fun with it, doing stupid things, laughing and getting the munchies. I still didn't believe I had a story like that. I didn't believe I had been hearing or seeing anything.

The day before I was due to be discharged we were outside having a smoke together.

Jacob asked: "Are you ever gonna smoke weed again, Clare?"

"Hell no", I said. "I never want to end up in here again."

"That's what I said too ... it's easy to say it in here," he said and the conversation trailed off, lingering with sadness.

When I came home after three weeks, suitcase in hand, Dad jokingly asked me: "You been on a trip, Clare?"

I laughed it off, as it was true, not merely just tripping out, but I had never really let go of travelling overseas. I knew then I had to accept I was home and get on with my life. Stop thinking about high school and boys, stop trying to fit in with people I shouldn't be hanging out with, stop smoking weed and just sort my life out.

WHAT MUM SAW

by Serena Kenyon

When Clare asked me to write my version of the events surrounding the two psychotic episodes which resulted in her being admitted to hospital, I was very reluctant to do so. Rather than being able to remember the details clearly, it is a period of her life (and mine) I had not wanted to think about much ... until now. I had kept all the sad feelings and emotions very deep within me and I hoped never to revisit them.

"Just a couple of paragraphs please, Mum, and can you finish it by next week?" was Clare's request to me. I wonder whom she was trying to kid? How do you compress that terrible time into a few paragraphs?

So I thought about it for a while. Meantime she kept on nagging me ... and I put it off. I didn't want to go back to that dark place in my memory. Clare was as proud as punch when she announced she'd finished writing her story. "So come on, Mum, can you get on with it, please, it won't take you long."

I knew I needed to read her story before I could write mine. But I didn't want to read it. I was scared of what it was going to reveal.

"Hanging out the dirty washing" ... isn't that what it's called?

So I read it. Wow, it was difficult to read and harder to take in. All sorts of questions sprang into my mind. Where WAS I during those years? How did it get that bad and why didn't I notice my daughter's unhappiness, her confusion and emotional problems? How did I not notice the drugs?

With the benefit of hindsight, lots of the very wrong sort of experience and a fair bit of new-found wisdom, I can look back at those years in disbelief and wonder why I was, to all intents and purposes, asleep at the wheel and didn't see her life unravelling until it was at crisis point.

Sometimes life sucks and shit happens. Our family has had a pretty large dose of it – and Clare's quite graphic description of how it was for her has shone the spotlight on those terrible years that came after my marriage to her father, Adrian, broke down following the collapse of our business.

All our three children have internalised those stresses and reacted to them in different ways and at different times in their lives.

But it's how we manage what happens to us that makes or breaks us, I think. From my point of view, I look at that time as a period of "major mismanagement" and there are big lessons for me to learn. Too late? I hope not.

So Clare has written her story as part of her healing journey. I wondered if writing about it might help me too.

In December 2007 we were so excited to see Clare and her boyfriend Jack home again after their overseas trip. She was like a breath of fresh air around the place. She looked wonderful and was confident and excited about the next phase of her life.

Her stories about the trip were tremendous and the photos were testament to a fun and exciting time. They had done so much.

PARTIES, PILLS & PSYCHOSIS

In her letters and emails, she hadn't elaborated on the difficulties and arguments she and Jack started having towards the end of the trip. Neither did we know they were going to break up when they got home. So it came as a shock. Sandra (Jack's mother) and I were very sad. Clare and Jack had simply grown apart.

Clare's nineteenth birthday party in February seemed like a turning point. She started going out with a boy called Nathan (I didn't know him at all, although they were at school together).

Clare enrolled at the University of Western Australia to do arts. She wasn't sure what subjects to choose or where it was leading, but she was keen to start.

But pretty soon it seemed to me she was becoming a bit scatty and rushed and disorganised, although she dismissed my concerns and enquiries as to whether everything was OK.

A bit later down the track she said she wasn't enjoying a couple of the subjects and felt very shy and intimidated in the tutorials. She would say things like "everyone else is smarter than me" – which I thought was an odd comment to make. But I understood how she felt – it had been like that for me at university too. So we talked about ways to cope better.

I noticed she began spending less and less time at university and not doing any work or study or assignments, but any comments I made were met with increasingly defensive rejections.

She was out most nights and every weekend. "Catching up with girlfriends" and "partying", I was told. "Don't worry, Mum, I'm fine" was the standard line to any of my enquiries as to her wellbeing.

I had a niggling "something isn't right, I don't really like this" feeling about this strange lifestyle. I couldn't put my finger on it and – heck – Clare had pulled off the most remarkable year. Maybe she was letting her hair down and would soon get stuck into university and her studies.

CLARE KENYON

Running parallel to all this, I still had much to think about with Charlotte. She was trying to complete Year 12 and her TEE. She was still very unwell and the stress I was feeling, having coped with her illness and now her recovery since Year 10, was relentless and exhausting.

Derrick started to bob into Clare's life and it gave me the creeps. This married man was showing an unhealthy interest in Clare, and Adrian and I told her several times of our concerns. Clare laughed us off and said he was just a friend, that they would go to the gym or go running together, but I saw something way more sinister developing. At that stage I didn't know Clare's friends also felt the same creepy thoughts about Derrick.

Clare was becoming less motivated and uninterested in university. She was terribly messy at home, chronically disorganised and distracted. She was rushing and busy in a hopelessly unproductive way. She was seeing a lot of Lucy – another girl from school whom I didn't know much about. She seemed to be drinking more and was smoking a lot – which totally grossed me out. Almost every weekend she would lose either her bankcard or ID because she was getting so drunk and one time, even her passport. But this she kept hidden from me as much as possible. My attempts to talk with her about the drinking and smoking were dismissed, and I was getting more concerned.

It was around the middle of the year when Adrian introduced Clare to the idea of internet marketing and share trading. Because of our dire financial situation, Adrian was full steam ahead on just about every business idea that came across the internet. He was desperate to try and salvage our lives.

I was less than keen – almost hostile, in fact – to the whole notion, but Clare went to a weekend seminar with her Dad and came away thoroughly fired up and enthused. She wanted to quit university and work this new business model, establish a good business, make money and be off travelling again. There was lots of squabbling and arguments, but in the end, that's what happened. She quit university. The idea of an overnight success would actually take several years to achieve (like most businesses do), but Clare was way too impatient and

PARTIES, PILLS & PSYCHOSIS

scatty to see that.

By now, Derrick was becoming a serious problem. I thought he was "grooming" Clare and wanted Adrian to ring his wife and spill the beans. I considered him a very sick sort of person to be trying to hit on a young girl. But Clare didn't see it like that and wouldn't listen to me … until Derrick did try and make a move and it scared the hell out of her and brought her to her senses.

I didn't know ANYTHING about the drugs Clare was now taking on a regular basis. I didn't know Christopher was involved in this either – I just didn't know a damn thing. How stupid could I be? Or how clever were these kids in hiding it from me? Most likely a bit of both.

Things were going pear-shaped in our house. Charlotte was having a serious health meltdown again, Clare and her Dad were arguing about the internet marketing business he had put money into, I was attempting to keep a home-based dog grooming business operating, and all the while Clare was displaying psychotic symptoms and we didn't know.

She was becoming very distracted, quite aggressive and defensive to our questions and her lifestyle was becoming "secretive" and strange. And the mess! My goodness, the mess.

To see a girl who had been so organised, diligent and focused on working, saving and planning for her overseas trip with Jack, turn into someone so forgetful, terribly disorganised and chronically messy was almost too painful for words.

Clare wasn't sleeping much either – something she did tell me. And she said she couldn't stop the constant chatter and thoughts in her head. Adrian would nod and say, "yes I have the same problem, Clare, over-thinking things". But I was very worried about this, especially when I found out she was spending hours on the computer. She didn't take any notice of my suggestions and requests to stay off the computer.

I did ask many times whether she was smoking dope but she denied it. I went further and broke the cardinal rule of "preserving personal space" and rummaged through her room a couple of times (this was no easy task, let me tell you; in fact, I could have disappeared under the clutter and heaving mess for days and no one would have found me).

I found a bong, lots of cigarettes, but no dope. When asked about this, Clare admitted she smoked some dope "only a bit at weekends at parties". And yes, I noticed her weird behaviour was at its height early in the week after partying all weekend. I took her to task about it, but was told, "Everything is OK, leave it Mum".

I knew Jack had smoked dope at school and I was pretty sure Clare had too – but I had no idea how much. I knew they smoked overseas, but for some inexplicable reason I didn't think it was a big issue back here. I rather thought it was a travelling thing and over and done with now she was back home. Hello! Hello! Wake up, Australia!

The crunch came at the Conscious Living Expo at Claremont Showgrounds in September 2008. Adrian and I were going for the day and Clare decided to join us. This was so strange because she was, by that time, never spending more than the odd few minutes in our company. So for her to want to spend a day out with us was completely out of left field.

But it was a bit like taking an ADHD toddler out for the day. She was "off with the fairies" – quite literally. Her speech was disjointed and muddled, she seemed confused and almost spaced out. She kept disappearing, and at one stage we found her in a darkened tent where there was chanting, incense, meditation, very strange music and lots of heaving sweaty bodies!

At home that evening, the strange "lights are on but absolutely no one is home" type behaviour was getting worse. Adrian and I didn't know what was going on but I was getting very scared and it was definitely time to go to the doctor. Clare was very sick, I knew that much. She was on her phone, on the computer, she was talking

PARTIES, PILLS & PSYCHOSIS

gibberish nonsense, and she was all over the place in her thoughts, speech and behaviour. It was getting very unpleasant and she was getting pushy and angry, bordering on aggressive.

I'm not at all sure how we got through that night. Clare was wide-awake and I followed her around as she paced the house and just couldn't settle. I couldn't get her to bed, she couldn't sleep, I just couldn't calm her at all. She said she was receiving messages from her computer, that voices were telling her to do things, that people were watching her. It was really scary stuff and freaking me out.

Hindsight is terrific, isn't it? Looking back, it was pretty obvious we should have taken her to emergency at Fremantle Hospital, but we were confused ourselves and rational decision-making goes out the door under these circumstances.

So next day we went to see our family GP. He suggested Clare was suffering psychosis and she needed to go to hospital. It was the first time I'd heard this word. He arranged an appointment at the Alma Street Clinic that same afternoon. Clare was agitated and uncooperative, restless, unable to concentrate, be still, or focus. But our GP seemed to have made her understand that her condition was serious, she needed help and she must attend the clinic with me.

Easier said than done! We headed off to Alma Street and we waited, for what seemed like an eternity, before doctors saw Clare and I was interviewed as well. Twice during the wait Clare announced she was leaving and would go to the door. Fortunately it was locked. She insisted she was OK, and didn't need to be at a hospital. It doesn't sound much, but it was very stressful and difficult trying to keep Clare in the waiting room.

Then for some inexplicable reason, the doctor told us to go home. There were no beds. We were to come back next morning to "try again" to be admitted. I was completely shocked and insisted on waiting in triage for as long as it would take. But they wouldn't allow us to stay; they gave Clare some medication (supposedly to calm her down) and sent us home. What a disaster!

CLARE KENYON

Less than four hours later, I was in the emergency waiting room at Fremantle Hospital with Clare going completely loopy. We were very quickly triaged into the emergency area. A doctor later told me she had suffered a psychotic episode – a nice neat description maybe, but it certainly wasn't "neat" to see or deal with. Nor was it any help during the next twenty + hours we spent in the emergency department until Clare was finally admitted to the hospital.

It was terrifying to be in this place and to watch Clare, who was so sick and distressed and completely out of control and to realise I didn't have a clue what was going on in her head.

A doctor gave her some drugs to calm her down and said we had to wait until a psychiatrist could admit her. The drugs helped a little. I later researched what they were. She would oscillate between a restless noisy sleep to a state of complete gibberish nonsense and high energy. She said people were watching her, talking about her, sending her messages. She couldn't make eye contact, she didn't like the bright lights so I turned them off, she was hearing voices, she would announce she was all right and nothing was wrong, get off the bed and charge out of the room before I would grab her and persuade her to come back. Nothing she said made any sense. Then she would burst into tears and the whole scene would be replayed.

The emergency department was full to overflowing with all manner of patients. Occasionally, a doctor or nurse would check on us, but I think they were relying on me to keep her quiet. Usual sort of stuff in an understaffed public hospital. So we waited.

Adrian came to sit with us for a while and then Charlotte came with some clean clothes and together she and I managed to access a bathroom and give her a shower. I'm a bit pushy like that. I'd been looking around the emergency section and had "spied" various facilities. I sort of "helped myself" to the bathroom, rather than ask if it was OK – but the nurses and doctors were so busy I guess they didn't really care as long as we didn't want them involved.

Finally, we were taken to Alma Street ward. What a hauntingly

PARTIES, PILLS & PSYCHOSIS

ghastly place this is – a small room at the end of a corridor completely devoid of anything remotely "homely or nice". This would all make sense to me later as I realised how careful doctors had to be with very sick patients on suicide watch, but first sightings and impressions were awful. A nurse came to see Clare and I was asked to leave. Just like that.

Hello! Didn't anyone want to know what I knew? Apparently not.

Back home I went on the computer and researched psychosis and schizophrenia – the what, when, where, why and how. What else can happen and where to afterwards.

Oh my goodness, it made the most terrifying and scary reading. I was completely overwhelmed with fear for the future and whether Clare would fully recover. I didn't think it could get much more serious than this. I felt completely helpless and lost, and cried and cried. I remember trembling with fear and not knowing what to do next.

Sometime later, Clare called me. She had her period, and would I bring down some sanitary stuff. The last time I had seen Clare she was with a nurse in her room. Now as I went down the corridor and found it empty, a wave of anxiety spread over me. At the nursing station I asked where she was. Directed to "out that door and over there somewhere", I found Clare sitting at a table with a male patient. This was obviously the smoking area – I could barely catch my breath for the stink. I wasn't at all prepared for what I saw. An area with half a dozen men and women, in all sorts of states of disrepair (for want of a better word), it was noisy, it felt quite threatening, and there was Clare at a table, smoking and laughing with a very less than desirable looking person.

I had it in my perhaps naive mind that now Clare was in hospital, she was going to be looked after, that she was going to be safe, but here was this quite different looking scene to what I presumed it should be like. I was shocked and lost for words. I handed over the sanitary items to her, mumbled a goodbye and left, feeling completely flustered and confused.

CLARE KENYON

Back in my car I sat there, trying to figure it out. What was I feeling? Shame? Guilt? Fear? Confusion? Terrible, dark sadness, that's for sure. Welcome to the world of the WA mental health system, Serena; it was time to get a grip and toughen up.

Clare has a different and simple interpretation of that same event and I was interested to read her version. It was one of acute embarrassment – a "how COULD you give me that stuff in front of everyone, Mum" moment.

But for me it was very different. From the comfortable hotel-style setting of the private hospitals Charlotte had been in for treatment, I was now in a government-run hospital in all its ugliness and rawness, treating – and as it should be, of course – all-comers, with the most serious of mental health symptoms. The patients with psychosis and schizophrenia – with the same symptoms as Clare. This was a very sobering moment for me and it made an enormous impact. This was my reality now. Clare was no different from any of these people and she was right there amongst it all.

Mental illness is completely indiscriminate. People from all levels of society become ill and need care and treatment. I'd seen some pretty confronting and desperately sad things during the time Charlotte was in hospital and I thought I had a pretty tolerant and empathetic outlook towards mental health sufferers.

But the patients at Alma Street were to ratchet this up to a whole new level – this was lesson No. 1 for me.

Lesson No. 2 would come later – when I learned that ONLY government hospitals with emergency departments would treat patients with acute psychotic symptoms or those having a complete breakdown. Private psychiatric hospitals and clinics won't touch these patients with a ten foot pole – they are too potentially dangerous, too unstable and too "not nice". But I digress.

Clare was in Alma Street for almost four weeks. At first she seemed not to take any of her treatments, group therapy sessions or patient programs very seriously. It was almost as if she thought none of it applied to her and she was just there for the ride.

She's pretty smart and I think she had the doctors and nurses well bluffed into thinking she was OK and didn't need to be in hospital at all – that sort of thing. I think she had worked out the answers to the doctors' questions so they heard what they wanted to hear.

Her medication dosage wasn't excessively high, apparently. We were kept well briefed by her doctor; the nurses were helpful, attentive and quite caring.

Our family had got into a routine of visiting her every evening, joining the group of patients (and sometimes their family or friends) in the bleak communal eating area. There was a small pool table in one corner, a broken down piano in the other, a shelf full of puzzles with pieces missing, card games with cards missing, out-of-date magazines and an appalling lack of books. Then there was the sink, the cheap and nasty coffee and tea, the urn and the mess. There was absolutely nothing nice or conducive to healing about this place. The food would make anyone sick, I reckoned. The picture is imprinted on my brain for life, I think.

But there was gradual improvement. Clare's mind slowed, as did her speech; her voice pitch increased in volume and tone, her thoughts began to clear a little, the sentences started happening again instead of just words, her eyes focused, she could sit and be still for more than a couple of minutes. The paranoia was fading. She was settling back into her own skin. She was calming down. But there was little acceptance by her of her situation. She just wanted out.

About two weeks into her stay, the doctors, in their great "wisdom", decided she was well enough to come home for a few days – the idea being that if all was well she could be discharged! Adrian and I were pretty shocked. There was absolutely no way she was well enough. "How silly were these people", I thought.

So there we were, with this ADHD-like nineteen-year-old in our home. She didn't know where to put herself or what to do with herself. Scatty as. And she was scared too. Away from the hospital, the routine, the security she had only half-accepted, she found herself a bit fearful and nervous. So next day, at her instigation and my insistence, we went back to the hospital.

I think there was a big shift in Clare's thinking after this event. A family friend is a senior social worker at Alma Street and had an overarching and supervisory involvement in the hospital therapy sessions and programs. Clare started scheduling regular talks with her, she participated more in therapy sessions, and she appeared to be taking it more seriously now, like it DID apply to her after all. She was slowly getting better, but we had no idea (and no one was telling us) just how long it was going to take. That was for us to find out along the way.

When it was time for her discharge, we had a "family meeting" with the doctor and social worker. We talked about her medication schedule, what she could and couldn't do, what she should and shouldn't do, follow-up weekly visits by the first psychosis group social worker. It sounded pretty good. Jeepers, I was nervous.

How was it going to be at home? I had customers coming every day for dog grooming, Adrian was away at work a good deal of the time, Charlotte was heavily focused on her TEE and the end of her schooling. Clare's friends were studying at university and into exams or working full-time – it looked like I was "it".

It wasn't like Clare could relax with a good book. Her concentration span was still very poor; she couldn't focus on the words for more than a couple of minutes. Such a difference – Clare had always been a real bookworm and loved reading. It was tricky.

The next little hurdle we came to as she continued to feel a bit more grounded and calm in her mind was she wanted to stop taking her medications and discontinue her outpatient appointments with the doctor. She was very impatient to "do something".

PARTIES, PILLS & PSYCHOSIS

"I don't need this stuff anymore, Mum, it's making me put on weight and it makes me tired," she said.

I suppose it's testament to the good, solid relationship that Clare and I have that she kept taking her meds and moving forward to get better. Sure we argued, we discussed, we disagreed – but ultimately she did as I asked and she continued to take them. She could have refused, arguing "she was an adult now and could do what she liked" – but fortunately it wasn't like that in our case.

However, it's not like that for many people. Many radio interviews and reports I've listened to since this time have brought it home so clearly this is a fragile period in the recovery of mental health patients. They feel better, they think they are OK, they stop taking their meds and they quickly relapse. In the absence of family or medical support so many sufferers fall off the medication bandwagon.

Adrian and I learned quickly that the very LAST people to acknowledge or understand they are really, really sick – are the sick people themselves. Clare was no different. She just didn't get it. Her reality was where she was at – at each and every stage of her illness and recovery. It's difficult to make them understand. Clare would be on a lowering dose of Rispiridone over twelve months before finally being discharged from hospital, as in no more appointments with her psychologist but she decided after about eight months that she simply would not take her medication and told her psychologist this too. She had decided she was all better.

FINDING ME AND FALLING IN LOVE

"I remembered the thump of the bass and the pump of the kick because my heart was almost out of my body. I felt free. I felt joy. I felt things I never thought I'd feel before."
Meat Katie – Divine

"Back once again with the ill behaviour, can you feel it, feel it nothing to save ya"
Ill Behaviour – Danny Byrd

Good Vibration Festival - February 2009

PARTIES, PILLS & PSYCHOSIS

Picking myself up after the hospital stay was tough. I wasn't really sure where I belonged, what to do, whom to talk to. I hadn't really adapted to life again when I returned home from my travels, I hadn't got over my "travel blues". My mind had been constantly distracted and absent from the now, remembering where I was, who I was with, what I was doing this time last year. I hated being at home again, where my brother was angry, my sister was struggling through Year 12 and Mum and Dad were forced to live together because they couldn't afford not to. I hadn't really fitted back in with my usual group of mates after having such a whirlwind time learning about the new me while over there. I had just been living this incredible life, surrounded by culture, art, music, beautiful architecture, scenery and energetic people, and so the predictability of day-to-day living got me down.

Looking back, I had been drunk or high since my return because life in Perth had become so mundane and such a disappointment. I had got into drugs because it was new and exciting. Now I had to face things properly and move on. It would be a fresh start.

I had a social worker who came to see me each week, and would talk me through my doubts and fears which helped a lot. Her name was Angela and I don't think I could have got my life together again without her. She knew I was writing a journal so she suggested I enter a writing competition through the hospital. I wrote a short story about my episode and recovery and won third prize.

I was still on medication – 2mg of Rispiridone, which was eventually reduced over time. They told me at the beginning I would have to be on this for several years. Unfortunately, the main side-effect was weight gain and I put on quite a few kilos which didn't help my self-esteem at all. But no matter how much I exercised it wouldn't come off.

It was clear I wasn't going to hang out with Nathan and his crew anymore because I didn't do drugs and we didn't want to be together anyway. I felt like they wouldn't want to be with a "mentally insane" girl anyway – those insecurities; worrying what other people thought, still fed back into my life every day. I would see Nathan out sometimes and I was able to explain what had happened to me, which felt like enough closure for me. He told me I had been acting weird, and I had often repeated my sentences and questions to him. I guess my mind was elsewhere and I wasn't concentrating. It was interesting to hear someone else speak about it, though, as I sometimes didn't believe it was true. But hearing it from another person other than Mum or my doctor made it real.

My girlfriends from high school – Cara, Sarah, Ana and Tahlia – weren't around because I had shunned them when I had started taking party drugs. I didn't think they were "cool" anymore because they didn't want to party like I did. Plus they hadn't wanted to hang around with me either. So I didn't know where to turn, I felt like I didn't have anyone and there was no one else to blame but me.

Fortunately, Lucy stayed close by. She had come to see me in hospital and said she understood when I said I wouldn't smoke weed again. She seemed more scared by the situation than I did. I think it was then she was thinking about breaking up with Liam. Tom brought me flowers and came to see me a couple of times, he took me out CD shopping when I wasn't allowed to drive and was just generally a mate I could count on, which I was so grateful for. Those people were there, but my illness left me feeling like I was an outcast, that no one understood me, and it was so hard to talk about as I didn't fully understand it myself. It was very lonely at the time.

The hospital stay gave me a major reality kick, a second chance at health. I realised how stupid I had been and all I wanted was to be happy again. The one thing that changed was the urge to hear that music again. Those few nights I had with the boys and Lucy at drum n bass gigs, Good Vibrations and Future Music festivals, opened my eyes, and now I could never forget. Something about it drew me to it. It was the first time in my life I felt free and alive, in Perth, at home. Little did I know it would grow into my passion and my reason for living.

I was working at a café four days a week, trying to figure out my next move. I didn't really want to go back to university as I had no idea what to study. I searched the internet every day for jobs. There were heaps of adverts for travel agents and I thought that would be perfect.

PARTIES, PILLS & PSYCHOSIS

I loved to travel and I knew so much about the world! Plus $540 a week seemed like a lot of money at the time. I applied for many jobs but never got any calls.

When the end of the year came round I was in such a state of confusion, Mum ultimately made the decision for me. She came into my room one morning – she knew I had been crying.

"Clare," she said, "why don't you just go back to university and do a couple of units, just for interest, make some new friends and then reassess at the end of the year?"

I nodded, it sounded OK to me. I enrolled in psychology, linguistics and anthropology and took a French course outside university. I loved using my brain again, loved feeling smart. My confidence had been blown the year before, working stoned and feeling stupid as a checkout chick where I couldn't even process a refund. Here I was around thinking minds again. I made a couple of friends at university, went to a few of the parties and joined EMAS (the Electronic Music Appreciation Society) where I was getting free DJ lessons. By the end of summer 2009 (March), I was feeling much better.

Over that summer as I was finding my feet again, I became a lot closer with Lucy, Jessy and Cory. We became a foursome and did everything together. I felt happier than I had in a long time. I stuck to the promises I had made to my parents and my doctors ... for a while. But once the festival season started again I got back into it. And it was quite by accident ... or was it?

We were going to Parklife festival (29 September 2008), and had pre-drinks at Cory's house. Tom spoke up and said: "Whatever you do, guys, don't give Clare any drugs today."

I just laughed ... "Tom, I will be fine", and I was a little embarrassed over this unwanted attention.

Mum was worried when I left the house but Tom picked me up and reassured her he would look after me. And I had every intention of going drug-free at the festival; also, I was scared of what might happen.

The festival was great fun, I was so happy to be back in amongst things. But my medication made me very lethargic and I could hardly dance, even though I had been drinking Red Bull. I was sitting with a couple of girls I had just met, just chatting. Tom wasn't with us. I was looking around at everyone running amok and unknowingly said out loud to myself, "I wish I had a pill". A girl turned and looked at me. "I'll get you one," she said. Fifteen minutes and $20 later a pink heart was in my hand.

Not letting myself think twice I swallowed it. And I had one hell of a night. I remembered the feeling, the rush, the intensity, not giving a fuck what anyone thought because everyone loved you and you loved everyone, and of caring only about the night. My whole body had been elevated into a whole other world of feeling good. There was no paranoia, no racing mind, and no weird thoughts. I just felt amazing. The doctors had no idea what they were on about. I went home safe and sound with Cory and Lucy.

After that, we all unconsciously accepted I was OK and started to party harder together again. I never really explained it to Cory and Lucy – it was easier to put it out of our minds and blame it on weed. Jessy wouldn't take any drugs, so she was unofficially our "sober driver". Fuelled by our love of the music and dancing, we went to gigs most weekends and every festival of the season. Over the summer of 2008/2009, I spent about $4500 on tickets, gigs, drugs and booze.

It's hard to describe the feeling at a festival when you are seeing an amazing DJ set surrounded by thousands of people cheering, laughing, talking and dancing; as you look over to your best friends and catch their eyes, you grin knowing - they are loving it just as much as you. We would laugh at the way each of us looked and acted on pingerz[14] – gurning[15] , talking rapidly and breathing hard – we laughed at our dilated pupils and how deep our conversations could get sometimes; it was all just one big joke to us and everyone else that we met and partied with out in clubs and at festivals.

PARTIES, PILLS & PSYCHOSIS

I stopped taking my medication at this time as well. I wanted to shed myself of any memory of the hospital. I didn't want it to exist anymore. I had finally found happiness, joy and contentment, a place I fitted in, where I belonged and felt safe. I didn't feel comfortable in the clubs in Fremantle, all the girls dolled up and the guys hungry for sex. I didn't like the music at most of the big popular nightclubs as I was frustrated with the cheesiness of mainstream top 40 music and the shit the lyrics talked about. I felt artists in the commercial pop industry were more of a marketing product than creatively talented and I couldn't relate or enjoy their music. I didn't like dancing to it one bit. So the first time I went to Barrick, an underground breakbeat nightclub in the city, I wanted to yell out, "I'm home". The vibe, the energy, the tunes were so good I became a little obsessed.

There the local DJs spun their own tunes as well as tracks I had never heard before and would probably never be able to find on the internet, it was that underground. This music wasn't about making money, but it was about dancing and having a good time, and you could tell the DJs were passionate about that. The club opened me up to different genres such as breakbeat, electro-house, tech-funk, booty-breaks, ghetto-funk, tech-house, deep-house, just to name a few. Cranking tunes would be playing all night and everyone in the club would be there for the love of the music, for their love of the underground. It was a small club and it had an intimate feel, as if you were a part of something special, a family. Not even on drugs, the music got me going like nothing had before. The bass drop invaded my senses and it became part of the addiction of it all. Lucy and Cory loved it too, so we kept going back.

The drum n bass scene in Perth was big and Lucy and I went to as many gigs as we could. Drum n Bass appealed to me like nothing ever had before, the party lifestyle was attractive and my world was constantly exciting. I lived and breathed dance music and I lived only for the weekend. All my money was spent on gig tickets, drugs, alcohol, party dresses, kicks[13] and taxi fares. Life existed only between gig dates, and that period of 10 pm - 6 am on the weekends was all that mattered to us. I became quite snobbish about the dance music scene and would only ever talk to guys who were into it. And it was yet another thing that took me further into the drug scene and away from my high school girlfriends, who were studying hard to get their degrees.

I didn't have to prove myself with Lucy, Cory and Jessy. They accepted exactly who I was and what I liked. I had convinced myself that weed was the problem, that it caused my paranoia and psychosis. It was linked to why I was down and unmotivated in Year 11 and, taking only ecstasy as I now did, I was fine – it all made perfect sense to me. I was nineteen and pretty naïve and I didn't really understand the severity of my illness or the permanent effect it could have on my brain. To me finding a place I was comfortable in was more important – it's what everyone craves. I didn't feel self-conscious on ecstasy, I wasn't afraid to do anything. I lost weight once I was off the medication and my confidence was growing. I liked being with Lucy, Cory and Jess because it seemed like they didn't care what anyone thought and so I stopped being so insecure as well.

Lucy and I became partners in crime. Lucy was still dating Liam so drugs were fairly easy to get most of the time. We would get on ecstasy and dexies, racking up lines in cars before we went into a club, or in the toilets of the club. It became a bit of a joke because we would sit in the bathrooms, high, talking for what seemed like hours, then finally getting out to dance. We would dress up for raves and gigs, in army costumes, or in bunny ears for Easter weekends; glowsticks, lollypops and Vix nasal inhalers were out at every rave. We would discuss in great detail what we would wear to each festival for days beforehand. Lucy and I would sneak past security and get up on stage to dance at clubs and bars, we even tried it at some festivals and got kicked off almost every time. Lucy would grab my hand and push us through the crowd to get to the front for artists like Stanton Warriors, Armin Van Burren and Andy C. She would tap on random guys' shoulders to get them to lift us up – we were always guaranteed the best view. We were flirtatious girls, always getting guys to pay for our drinks. We would never wait in a toilet queue; we'd make best friends with people around us, and once the night was over, we spent the rest of the night talking about something deep and meaningful. I never laughed so much in my life than when I was out at music events

PARTIES, PILLS & PSYCHOSIS

with Lucy and Cory.

I loved having best friends to run amok with and have hilarious nights out with. I missed being close like this with a girl. Lucy was beautiful and I liked the attention I got from guys when I was with her. She gave me a whole new sense of confidence. We were young, wild and free nineteen-year-olds, completely living the moment without a care in the world.

Finding and sourcing pills for gigs and festivals was both annoying and fun. Fun because it was dangerous and exciting to talk about – you had to be careful what you said over text. We would have silly code words for things and it felt like it was our own little secret. Friends of friends of friends would be contacted when we got desperate, and then driving around to places and meeting up in car parks became part of the fun.

We laughed about the ways we would sneak drugs into a festival and loved the adrenalin rush of getting away with it. On one occasion, I was paid to carry 30 pills into a festival. I realise now I didn't really have a clue about the possible consequences, such as jail time. As we got closer to the event, we heard that sniffer dogs were out front and I started to panic. When we arrived, there wasn't a dog in sight and I breezed through the gates.

At this time, I was learning how to shuffle[16] – an underground dance move that can be seen in nightclubs and at raves. Ravers tend to wear partly fluorescent pants, known as Phat Pants and shuffle to hard style music – that is the actual Melbourne Shuffle, and not what pop band LMFAO made famous with their song Everyday I'm Shuffling. I taught myself to shuffle and how to stomp and as I have always been a very good dancer, I picked it up quickly and became very good at it. Slowly but surely, I was coming out of the shadows again. I was becoming a little raver.

By the time I turned 20 I had quit my café job as it was ridiculously monotonous work and a friend from high school got me a job at a record hi fi shop which I loved from the word go. I was working with a cool group of people, surrounded by music all day. Most of my pay was spent on CDs from the shop, and a work colleague DJ'd outside of work so we would constantly talk music. University, work and partying – that was my life. Normal and carefree.

I wanted to show how happy I was, how I felt back on track, and I wanted to express my new-found identity – so I got another tattoo. It's on my wrist, and is a music staff over a love heart – it signifies my love for dance music and the happiness it brought me and every time I look at it, it makes me smile.

Sunday April 5, 2009

Up to this point, I have never written a happy diary – one where I didn't dwell on the difficulties in my life and the people who have let me down. So I have decided it is time I did this, because I have never been happier than these past couple of months – not with Jack, not in a different home, not even overseas.

I have come to realise so much about the past and about myself, it's overwhelming. I feel like I've come into my own and I know myself better. I haven't run away when things got tough; instead, I turned to my friends – something I've never done before – and to my family. Finding people I can be myself around and have fun with has been everything to me. Back in high school I was always shy and afraid, and totally unaware of myself. I think getting sick helped me get rid of my demons with my family, my friends and myself and just chill out.

I was so miserable in high school, so hung up on what people thought. Now I finally feel OK with myself, I can be who I want to be. The bad decisions in the past I think have led me to the point where I can truly say I'm happy with the way life is. I'm not thinking about being anywhere else in the world. I'm living the now and I thought I should document this amazing feeling before it's over. And to tell you the truth, I think I deserve it.

Monday May 11, 2009

PARTIES, PILLS & PSYCHOSIS

Sometimes I start to feel myself getting a bit worried about life. Like will everything turn out the way you hope? At what point do you realise that it's not doing that? What if I go through life and nothing spectacular happens? What if I am lonely forever and don't meet the man of my dreams? Will I be happy in ten years' time? My parents have pounded into me that money equals happiness, so I worry about what if my trading doesn't work. I think that deep down I believe it will and I let myself dream away with the possibilities of a rich life. The future scares me so much, though. I want so much for my family to be happy. I think I have come into my own this year. I don't have half the self-doubt I did have one, two, three years ago. I don't feel caught up, restrained, contradicted, confused. I like who I am.

Tuesday June 2, 2009

I feel like I'm at a bit of a crossroad again with university and life. I feel the pull, the attraction of earning more money, getting a full-time job. Being a travel agent will let me travel too. I want to be able to afford to party even harder than I do now because that's where I feel most free. Sure there are drugs, there's alcohol but when I'm listening to that music, dancing hard, laughing loads, it's all I ever want to do and I feel like everything else will eventually fall into place. I'm so lucky to have a friend like Lucy. I really don't know what I'd do without her. I'd be very bored, that's for sure. It's weird, I feel like she and Cory and Jess, especially over summer, helped me to find myself after the hospital and all of that last year. I do worry that Mum might find out I'm taking E again and stop me from hanging out with Lucy. It's not that she influences me anymore – we're probably as bad as each other. I don't feel like I'm doing anything "bad" or "wrong"; in fact, I feel like a normal young girl – one who is embracing life. But I feel like Mum sort of knows. How could she not when I come home looking like I do every weekend? I want to tell her, it's like this whole part of me she doesn't know and I hate lying to her all the time. How can parents accept alcohol and drinking but not the loveliness of ecstasy? It just makes people happy. No one fights each other on pingerz like you see drunk people doing on TV.

I have to think about my decisions thoroughly, though. Am I just repeating the same thing as last year? My parents don't know but really I quit university last year so I could party more and I used the business as an excuse. Am I doing that again? But then I think, isn't that telling me something? Isn't it telling me that the desire is so big it's always going to feed into my studies, so I'll probably never do well? I think I should quit, I'm not an academic after all, and I should make the trading work. Will this screw up my life? No, the trading will work. And so why not have fun now, while everything is perfect?

Boys came and went, but no one special came into my life – until Dylan. I met him at a gig at Barrick Nightclub. I saw him from across the room and admired the way he was getting down and grooving, obviously listening and caring only about the music. I wandered over and said hi. It was hard to talk over the thumping bass, but I caught a few things ... I think he was trying to impress me.

"I'm a DJ," he said, "here, at the club. Have you heard of Haven?"

"Yes," I replied, even though I hadn't a clue what he was on about.

It was a night at Barrick run by a few DJs.

"You should come and see me some time," he said.

I smiled and nodded, and we hooked up and danced together for the rest of the night. He gave me his number at the end and I texted later, saying it was nice to meet him and some flirty thing about DJ lessons. He then found me on Facebook and we chatted occasionally over the next four months, sometimes a text to see if one or the other was out. He was 22 and worked at a car retail shop but he dreamt of being a producer. It wasn't until July 2009 that we organised to meet up ... on a Saturday night at Barrick again.

I was out with Cory and Jessy. Cory and I had a pill before getting to the club. Dylan came about an hour later, said hello and gave me a kiss on the cheek. He looked so cute with his baseball cap on. I had such a

PARTIES, PILLS & PSYCHOSIS

thing for guys in caps. I loved the badboy look.

"Are you getting on any biccies[17] tonight?" he asked me.

"I've already had one," I answered.

"Oh, I'd better catch up then!" he said laughing.

We were standing at the bar by then waiting for drinks, and I watched him raise his arm and pop one in his mouth, in view of everyone. I laughed, I liked how this guy was so free, didn't care what anyone thought. We spent most of the night outside in the alleyway chatting. We really got along well and acted like we were already together, joking about what we would get up to together, like the local football derby as we went for opposing teams.

"You're cool," he said, "I want to see you again."

I felt giddy with happiness. Someone liked me, the new me, the fun me, the party me. The next week he texted me every day, and asked me out for a date on Friday night. We caught up for drinks and that's when we realised we connected, and we weren't on drugs this time.

I remember the whole night – our conversation would always revert back to music. We discussed drugs at length too. I was a little nervous about it, my past lingering in the background but I wanted him, so I didn't care at that point. Hell, I had been on it for almost a year since and I was fine, so it must have just been weed. This was my world now, or at least starting to be. I was addicted to this fast-paced, dangerous, exciting life. But I was honest with him; I didn't want to pretend I was something when I wasn't. I told him I had had a drug-induced psychotic episode from smoking weed and he seemed to understand what that meant and that I just didn't smoke it anymore.

A week later he invited me to see him DJ at Barrick. I was so excited, Lucy came with me and I bought a new little black dress for it and felt gorgeous. After saying hello, he immediately asked me to be his girlfriend. I was shocked! But of course I said yes, then he went around introducing me to his friends as "his new girlfriend". I was laughing and smiling the whole time. I couldn't believe it; someone this sexy and cool could like me!

From then on we developed a close relationship. I was at his house on Friday night and I wouldn't leave until Monday morning. Wednesday night was our date night too where we would cook dinner together, drink red wine, chat and watch TV. It was so normal, so couple-y, I loved it. Weekends became benders of highness, drunkenness, dancing, tunes, laughter and hangovers. We would get into clubs and gigs for free, I met lots of cool people in the scene and broadened my musical knowledge … the lifestyle was all so much fun.

After about two months, we were at Barrick, and I could feel Dylan watching me dance. I turned to him and caught his eye. He was smiling differently and he whispered in my ear, "I think I love you." I laughed and said, "We'll see when you're not on ecstasy". But he said it again later that night, and I said it back, and from there we were set. I was a smitten twenty-year-old girl.

I loved Dylan like something chronic. He was fun, sweet, gorgeous, funny and we got along so well. He quickly became all I thought of, all I really cared about and we talked like there was a future for us. The nights he DJ'd at Barrick were always something we looked forward to the most. I liked mingling around and meeting people, dancing and listening to his set, knowing full well he was coming home with me. I liked it when girls dancing next to me would turn to me and say, "isn't that DJ amazing, and he's so cute", and I would answer back, "Yeah, he's my boyfriend," and they would gush at how lucky I was. And I felt I was too, I thought Dylan was pretty amazing.

His passion for music and his desire to be a producer were things I admired. He would sit at the computer for hours trolling Beatport (online music store) and making tunes on Cubase (digital audio workstation). Dylan and Joe, the guy he shared his house with, were breakbeat-obsessive, their track list was endless, with numerous boxes of vinyl, and hundreds of CDs and mixes. They would be on the decks every night and day, and were exceptional. It constantly felt like a party,

PARTIES, PILLS & PSYCHOSIS

even during the week, when they mixed. Dylan had an ear for good tunes and could really get a crowd pumping. Their music knowledge was amazing and I learned so much when I was with them. I really was in heaven, surrounded by music at their house. I tried my hand at mixing a few times, but he was the DJ and I preferred to be the dancer.

The music was infused with the thrill of being in love, the highness of taking drugs and my joy in dancing. In a sense I had fallen in love but had fallen back in love with drugs as well, and what happened to me the year before no longer existed in my mind.

Monday September 7, 2009

I've let myself fall in love and it is the most wonderful feeling. I am so incredibly happy, on the first anniversary of the worst and scariest thing that ever happened to me. Dylan is the most perfect guy and he totally gets me. He is so sweet and funny and he spoils me rotten. I am the luckiest girl alive and I want to do everything I can to make him happy.

SEX , DRUGS, BREAKBEAT AND HEARTBREAK

"We live the party life, so get drunk, take drugs, make love and we'll do it all again tomorrow night, 'cause rain hail or shine these are the days of our lives, let's waste 'em away one day at a time"
Horrorshow - The Party Life

Pre-party - Mayhem Festival November 2010)

I fitted in with Dylan's crew straightaway, as they were all so welcoming, fun and friendly party people. Dylan lived with two other boys and their house was the pre-party house, the after-party house and the one where everyone would crash. We called it Club Redcliffe. The house had three bedrooms and one bathroom, and was broken down and old. It had a large backyard area with a shed, a few bad lemon trees and a crumbling brick fireplace outside. It smelt of cigarettes and weed and had liquor stains on the carpet. There was a small TV room with couches that didn't match and a dodgy bathroom with a mouldy shower curtain. The kitchen was the real living area, a big room with a large dining table in the middle with the boys' decks set up and mammoth speakers to one side. This is where everyone would hang out. It was a real boys' house. It might not sound too nice, but we all loved it.

PARTIES, PILLS & PSYCHOSIS

I wish I could remember every weekend there, I wish I could remember all the hilarious conversations we'd have at 4am with the fire going and the music cranking. I felt at home there; somewhere where I was free to be me without any judgement. And I forgot about all my issues, responsibilities and problems for those long hours we partied. Most of Dylan's friends smoked cigarettes and they all smoked weed as well. A lot of weed. I didn't want to make it an issue, so I didn't, and I knew what I was getting into at the beginning. It was uncomfortable at first explaining to them why I didn't want a bong when it was passed around because there would always be questions. They'd say things like "oh yes I know someone who tripped out too," and laugh in a way that made it sound like it was something funny. And in the end it was easier dealing with it that way.

Over the summer, I had quit smoking cigarettes, but I started again after dating Dylan for a while. It was just too hard when everyone around me was smoking, and yes I was very easily influenced. Smoking soon became something we needed while high and a sanctuary when coming down.

Dylan and I partied hard together, along with his friends but in particular his roommate and best friend Joe. Almost every weekend we would get on something, mostly pills, and get wasted. We would stay up on Friday night until we dropped on Sunday evening … literally. Sometimes I would have to pick Joe up off the table after he had passed out and drag him to bed. The boys would throw parties where they would DJ and everyone would be dancing and talking, and lines would be handed around on plates. We would play endless games of Jenga and build card pyramids while high, sitting and laughing around the kitchen table until the sun came up. Random people would be invited over for a kick-on after a big night at Barrick and wouldn't leave until next afternoon when the sun was falling back down again and reality was sinking in that real life had to begin again.

Dylan and drugs opened up the world of sex for me as well. Never in my life had I felt so sexy, wanted and beautiful when we were together. I was always a little insecure with Jack, sexually, and just with myself in general. But now I felt like I could let myself be vulnerable to

Dylan and it was OK. We explored each other, most of the time when we were high which made it that much more intense. Sometimes we would go at it for what seemed like hours, which is another attraction of being on drugs. We would pause briefly to share a cigarette and then continue on. We were so comfortable around each other. We would spend what felt like hours in the shower together, letting the hot water wash all over us. Dylan loved to be the little spoon and I'd give him massages on his shaved head, he would tickle me until I was crying with laughter and we would play-fight and wrestle until we were both exhausted from laughter. We would stay up late together, me wrapped up in his big hoodie jacket and we would talk all night or just lie there together.

Tuesday December 1, 2009

I have been having amazing weekends with Dylan, we party so hard together. We are together through the intense highs and the lazy lows and each time I feel we fall in love that little bit more. I cannot express my happiness at the moment. A couple of weekends ago I teased him about being a drug addict and he teased me back saying, "You are too." I didn't feel sick or worried or disappointed in myself, I actually had a tingle of excitement rush up my spine. I love being in this world where it is OK and fun to do these things. I smiled back at him and said, "Yeah, I guess you're right". No way am I out of control, but it feels good to know I am not in conflict with myself like I was in Europe; it's good to accept myself.

I said goodbye to Angela today. I was and still am sad. She is such a nice person and I loved it every time she came round. Just talking to her every couple of weeks helped me so much because I could never lie to her. I trust her and she's honest with me. I told her I was taking drugs again and because nothing had happened she seemed to be OK with it. She was warning me for sure but not going crazy like Mum would. It's so surreal that this is all over and is actually in the past. Mum said she was proud of me. I have come a long way and I will never let her down again. This is the happiest I've ever been. Goodbye psychosis, high school, weed, paranoia, the hospital, the old me. Hello Dylan, friends, life, love.

PARTIES, PILLS & PSYCHOSIS

One night we had come home after a big night at Barrick and the boys, as usual, were smoking weed. I watched them, wishing I could just have a bong again and for it to be normal, missing the smell and the taste, wanting to join in on the session.

I said to Dylan, "if I have one and something goes wrong, just put me to bed ... what could go wrong really?" and he handed it to me without a second thought. But of course after two bongs, after nothing for a year, I was so stoned and so out of it. At first I was giggly but then paranoia came back in flashes, I'm not really sure exactly what happened that night but it was weird, it felt like I was right back a year ago where I thought the whole world hated me, including my boyfriend. And I ran away the next morning. I called Jessy to pick me up and left Dylan's house quickly, leaving him with a confused and sad look on his face.

After much thought I wrote him a letter, as it was the only way I could get everything I wanted to get out in one go. I told him no matter how high I was, how confident I seemed, he should never ever give me weed again. I told him it was a time I never wanted to experience again and I never wanted to feel like that again. He finally understood the seriousness of the situation and from there we were OK. But I continued to play with fire, still convincing myself it was just weed.

I tried a few drugs with Dylan for the first time. Coke and speed were some of them, but our main drug of choice remained ecstasy and dexies. They were into pharmaceuticals as well, benzos mostly, which make you feel relaxed, sort of stoned and silly if you stay awake. I got a prescription for Temazepan from my doctor as well, as we usually needed them after big nights, especially after a scary acid trip I had once which I couldn't come down from. The first time I tried acid was after a party Dylan and Joe threw. We were sitting around out the back, the sun was blazing, it was about 7am but none of us felt like sleeping after being on pingerz all night.

Someone must have called Dylan or Joe, because Dylan turned around to me and said: "Do you want to go around to where Crazy Pete is? He's got acid." I thought about it only briefly; the curious, rebellious party girl in me jumped up immediately and said yes.

A couple of minutes later we drove round the block and walked in on another party. There were about 20 people there, all of them drunk and high, and some had passed out on the couches. We bought the acid cubes, $20 each, and placed them on our tongues. They were liquid acid within a sugar cube, rather than a tab, and they dissolved almost instantly. We both looked at each other grinning.

Back at Dylan's we waited for them to kick in. Crazy Pete, Joe and two others, who were just passers-by for the day, had also taken them and we all sat around the kitchen table, not really talking, kinda just looking around. Then Crazy Pete spoke up: "Can everyone see that painting over there?" We all looked and suddenly started giggling, as it was moving and warping.

"Whaatttheeefuccckk," said Crazy Pete.

"Ha ha, that's so cool!" I said.

We had all started tripping and were having the exact same trip. Then it came on more strongly and we were all laughing – couldn't stop laughing – and we became fascinated with simple things. We were looking around and pointing at things in the kitchen as magnets on the fridge were moving around; the floor turned into water as it swirled around and an overwhelming feeling of highness came over us.

Eventually we all moved outside, staring up at the sky, the ground, the fire and coals as everything was still moving and then we slowly stopped talking and passed out in the sun. I had heard so many bad stories about tabs so I wasn't sure if I would ever try them; but this liquid stuff was really chilled and we had it a couple more times. The last time was enough for me when we double-dropped and I got very paranoid, to the point where I could not speak or move. So I took three sleeping pills to get to sleep. From then on I said to Dylan I would never do it again, though he did try to get me to on a few occasions.

The first time I tried speed we were at an awesome party up in the

PARTIES, PILLS & PSYCHOSIS

hills. One of Dylan's friends threw a cocktail party for his birthday. The place was heaving by the time we got there, as we were late from going to Dylan's Christmas work function. On the way there we joked about how sensible we looked at dinner, sucking up to Dylan's boss. Now we were going to get wasted.

People were spilling out the front as we walked in; the music was cranking and cocktails were in abundance. The house was situated on top of a hill, so there was an incredible view towards the twinkling city lights. It was a little broken down, but had an amazing backyard with plants and flowers, it was where everyone was hanging out.

The cocktails weren't really cocktails – people were already wasted by the time we got there, so any thought of making normal ones didn't come into it. Everyone was just throwing whatever they could find into blenders – all different spirits, juice, soft drink and fruits. Once blended, they came around in big jugs and everyone tried them. They were awful but we drank them anyway. Dylan had got a couple of dexie capsules so we went into the bathroom to rack them up. There was a huge amount of powder inside when Dylan split them open and he had such a huge line he started throwing up almost instantly. I had a smaller line and could soon feel the buzz and confidence kick.

After Dylan stopped vomiting we went outside and started to mingle. I lost Dylan eventually as I think he went to have a mix. I wandered around, chatting to all the people I was starting to get close to. There was Crazy Jules, who had the sweetest heart and made me laugh so much; Nat and Bradey, my favourite couple; my old pal Joe; and Max, Todd, Sky, Amy and Caleb. I was meeting many others for the first time and they would say things to Dylan like, "don't ever let this one get away". It made me feel so special.

After what seemed like a couple of hours, Dylan came over and whispered in my ear ... "I have a present for you". I had no idea what to think but he took me into a room where Caleb and Sky were sitting. He pointed at the table and this huge line.

"What is it?" I asked.

"Speed," he replied.

I grinned and rolled up a $20 bill. I snorted the line and looked up. I swear Dylan's eyes had a sparkle in them.

"Good, hey," he said.

All I could do was grin and nod.

It didn't take long to kick in. Suddenly the world was humming to a quicker beat. I couldn't stop smiling. I felt flirty, giggly, fun, energetic ... my body felt so good all over, alive and giddy. This feeling lasted the whole night and we were all dancing and giggling together, hugging and laughing. Sky told me I fitted into the group so well, and I was perfect for Dylan. It just added to the ecstatic feeling I was experiencing.

As the sun came up, the crowd started to disperse and there were about ten of us left and a few who had passed out. All the couches had been moved outside to the back, so we were all lazing around watching the sun come up, smoking and talking shit. I snuggled up with Dylan on one of the couches. I felt so comfortable and happy and wished the feeling would never leave and that nights like this would never end. When I had sobered up, I left Dylan there and drove home as it was Stereosonic festival (November 29, 2009) and I was heading to Lucy's for pre-drinks.

Another rave, more drugs, more dancing. Lucy and I had scored some white smileys for the day. Deadmau5 headlined and we stayed at the back watching his set. I told Lucy about my experience the night before. She grinned but I could tell she was starting to get worried about me, starting to think I was getting in over my head.

"Just promise me you won't do crack," she said.

"Don't worry, I won't, that's where I draw the line," I told her.

That summer was the time of gin and tonics and the blow-up pool. After work on the weekends I would scooter over to Dylan's and walk

PARTIES, PILLS & PSYCHOSIS

around the back where he and Joe would be sitting in the pool with beers.

"There's something inside for you, Clare," Joe would say, "help yourself."

I walked into the kitchen and bass filled my ears. The speakers were smashing out breakbeat splendour and I could see a couple of lines on the table with some notes nearby. I stopped for a moment, looked around the house, felt the music invade my body and smiled. I sighed and could not wipe the grin off my face. This place was home. I loved everything about it. I had a couple of lines and made myself a gin and tonic and went to join Joe and Dylan in the pool. And we stayed there chatting and laughing until long after the sun went down.

While I was partying with Dylan I was getting through university as well. But I didn't enjoy it because I was broke all the time and couldn't afford to party. I was over learning about things I thought were irrelevant to my life, and would constantly argue with my parents as I felt I would not be able to get a job after getting an arts degree. I quit the record shop job in middle of the second semester as I was having issues with the friend who got me the job. I got a new casual job at a shoe store, which I loved, but it never gave me enough money as I could work only about twelve hours a week before it affected my student allowance from the government.

For the second semester I was studying linguistics, psychology and an economics unit and I was still working on the forex and commodities trading course. I couldn't wrap my head around the economics unit and fell asleep in most lectures or I just wouldn't go. I didn't even sit my final exam. By that time I had had enough of study and wanted to work full-time, so my weekends would be free for fun (not the most mature decision I ever made), but I couldn't stop imagining myself as a travel agent. I thought I had figured out what I wanted to do with my life and that was it. So after many fights with Dad, with him threatening to kick me out of home, I got my way and dropped out of university and enrolled at TAFE to do a six-month Certificate III in Retail Travel Sales to commence in the following year, early 2010.

Over the summer festival season I had a new crew to go with. And it was different because we didn't have to hide our drug use from our friends. Everyone was open about it, they all chatted and laughed about it and got excited at the prospect of getting high and dancing at a rave all day together. The one I was looking forward to most was Breakfest (December 26, 2009) as I had never been before. Dylan wouldn't shut up about it as the day drew near.

We organised a bus to pick us up from the pre-party at the house of friends in the hills, and about fifteen of us jumped in drunk, high, and excited for the 45-minute journey to the venue. Lucy and her new boyfriend Ian came with us. They had got together about the same time as Dylan and I. Ian was also a local DJ.

The venue really makes this festival incredible, along with the vibe and good DJs. It's in a natural amphitheatre, which exaggerates the sound and looks unreal if you're either in the bowl looking up at the punters standing on the hill or up on the hill looking at the crowd raving in the bowl.

My first Breakfest was amazing for the music but scary because of the drugs. We had hooked up some brown stars which were speckled with orange. In the late afternoon when we dropped them, everyone threw up, including me, but for Dylan it was far worse – I think he had had more than a couple. He couldn't stop throwing up and his heart was racing like crazy; he felt so sick and was really out of it. I begged him to go to the ambulance and he finally agreed. We went and they were very cool about it all.

"What have you had?" they asked as they hooked him up to a heart monitor.

Dylan listed the substances and the ambos' eyes widened as they saw his heart beat rising and rising. They did some other test and told Dylan if they didn't have to stay at the festival they would be carting him off to hospital immediately as his heart was beating from the wrong valve or something. I was getting very scared for him, and also because I was on the same stuff.

PARTIES, PILLS & PSYCHOSIS

Eventually Dylan's heart calmed down and we took off to enjoy the rest of Elite Force. Dylan just lay on my lap while I watched the show. I messaged everyone to meet up after the festival and we caught the bus home. That night we experienced a horrendous come down and we weren't able to sleep a wink. Ian and Lucy stayed up smoking bongs with everyone. When Lucy passed out, Ian carried her inside, knocking her head on the doorframe. She didn't feel a thing or hear the rest of the crew laughing out loud.

Monday October 26, 2009

I went to Mayhem at Belvoir at the weekend, a local drum n bass festival with Lucy and Ian. It was so much fun - I was even shuffling on stage - right up until I saw a boy tripping out on something. He jumped up on to the stage ripped the decks off and attempted to hit the DJ before security came up and dragged him off. Later I saw him strapped down to a stretcher with a mask over his mouth. He was struggling, looking like he was crying out, wrenching against the restraints. It was the saddest, scariest thing I'd ever seen. What was in that boy's head, I wondered? What did he see on the stage or hear in his head? I knew the pain he was feeling. I wanted to hug him and tell him it would stop soon. I couldn't dance for the rest of the night. I couldn't stop thinking that that could have been me. I was on drugs at the festival; I had a couple of pills. What was I thinking? Dylan picked me up and I told him what had happened. He didn't understand, didn't say a word to comfort me. I guess he was confused, maybe didn't get why it affected me so much. I couldn't stop thinking about Mum and how she must have felt when I went crazy that night and was looping out in the emergency room. It's so hard to explain to people. I was somewhere else, I was being told things; being told to do things, say things, not being Clare. I was lost and scared. Dylan doesn't understand being out of control like that. No one does. I called Charlotte when I got back to Dylan's and I cried softly on the phone to her. She spoke to me until I calmed down.

"It's all OK, you're not in that place anymore and you're safe. You're safe," she said.

And I left that place again, removed it from my thoughts and went back to the kitchen to have a smoke with Joe and Dylan. I have blocked it out, but the world keeps reminding me that it's there. It won't ever leave me.

After the scare from Breakfest, and a big night on New Year's we went on a drug-break for a month or so, no pills, and we were also planning our holiday to Bali. My friends had all bought flights a couple of months earlier too, and my flight was my 21st gift from Dylan, who was coming on the trip with us. The lead up to the trip was so exciting. There were nine of us going together, Lucy, Cory, Sarah, Megan, Melissa, Aiden and Tahlia. We had booked a three-star hotel in Legian and because I was about to start my travel agent's course I was rushing around organising everyone and their insurance and making sure everyone knew what to do through the airport.

We got there and had an amazing ten days together. It opened up my eyes to how amazing Dylan was when it was just he and I together. He was so much fun and generous and sweet. We flew over to Jakarta together to meet his Dad, which was another eye-opener for me. His Dad was living a different but carefree, happy lifestyle, married to an Indonesian woman. Dylan hadn't seen his Dad for many years and he loved spending time with him and planned to go back in the middle of the year.

When we got home it was time for me to knuckle down and start my course at TAFE, and for Dylan to get back into work. He was working a 9-5 office job by then. It proceeded, but not with a great amount of enthusiasm. I was sick with a black cough for two weeks from chain smoking in Bali and there was my 21st party to plan for February.

My parents had not given my brother a party two years earlier because it was at the height of his binge drinking and anger issues and they didn't want to encourage "a piss up". So to keep it fair, they didn't want to throw one for me either. Dylan and Joe said I could have it at their house, so that was the venue and the music was organised. All I needed to sort out was booze. I wanted to have a beach-themed cocktail party as it was summer time. I got an all-you-could-drink slushie cocktails machine and spent a lot of money on decorations to

PARTIES, PILLS & PSYCHOSIS

make it look like a beach. Banners were put up around the fence in the backyard, there were blow-up palm trees and the blow-up pool was out in action too. Mum made the cake and food and we were all set to go for the night.

My friends came and their gift to me was $820, painted in a massive, novelty cheque. It was something they had all chipped in for, the purpose of which was to buy me a car. I couldn't have been more thrilled – I had been using a scooter to get everywhere and it made all journeys twice as long. Dylan and Lucy had sneakily organised the present behind my back. Also, my mates made me a Cuz.

Cuz is the nickname we call each other – i.e. "Hey Cuz", "Thanks Cuzin", "How you doing, Cuzzie?" Expressions like that. The Cuz they made me was a cardboard cutout of the letters and photographs of all of us stuck on them. It was one of the best, most thoughtful presents I've ever received and I keep it at my bed rest. Whenever I need a laugh I just have a look at it, as they are photos mainly of our nights out together. For everyone else's 21st after that we made a Cuz. Cara made me a scrapbook of our lives together since we were babies, which was the most beautiful thing anyone had done for me.

And among other presents, I was given a lot of free drugs later in the night. I was given about four dexies, a pill and a few lines of coke. It was probably the highest I had ever been. My brother came to the party, I was hoping in the back of my mind he would be proud of me, and think I was at least a little bit cooler than a couple of years ago, surrounded by the new mates I had and the scene I was in. When a neighbour came around in her pajamas about 7am the next morning, the party began to die down. Rather than pop her head over the back fence she walked around the entire block to ask for the music to be turned down down.

"Guys, I know it's someone's birthday," she said, "but it's Sunday morning, time to call it quits."

When she left we all burst out laughing.

CLARE KENYON

Tuesday March 2, 2010

Sunday night, and we hadn't been together for a while and we knew how much we wanted it. We were kissing for ages and it was incredible and passionate. It was 3am after lines of gear and he stopped suddenly and stroked my cheek and looked in my eyes for ages before saying, "I love you, Clare". It was so intense, my heart pounded like crazy. I don't get it – he tells me he loves me all the time but never like this, looking deep into my eyes, saying my name instead of baby or babe. I said it back but not quite the same as it took me by surprise. Dylan is amazing but that threw me – its intensity. I have the ability to break his heart as he does with me. I don't want the day to come when this ends. I'm not sure if I could recover. I'm not sure if I can love as much as I do now. Is it too early to say I want to spend the rest of my life with him? Is it possible to meet that person at 20 in a nightclub, who makes you feel alive and sexy, brave and scared at the same time? Someone who makes me laugh so much and tells me off for being too messy or forgetful, who calls me a clown but listens to me and understands what's in my head. I'm not afraid to be anything I want with him and when he holds me I feel like I'm in the safest place in the world.

But our relationship did not stand the test of time, for after a while, my love for him could not outweigh the issues we had. As the months went on, the honeymoon period ended and it really tested us. We started to fight a fair bit, he was jealous of a new friend I had made while out clubbing. His name was Jayden and he was a shuffler I had kept in contact with. Dylan hated me shuffling, told me I was showing off and basically ruined it for me while I was dating him. I was starting to get sick of Dylan smoking weed all the time and not doing anything else. Because I didn't smoke it anymore, I could see how it made people lazy and unmotivated. He would never go to the beach with me, or to a movie, take me out for dinner, or go for a walk, nothing. It just seemed like he didn't want to make any effort at all. When eventually I did convince him to go to the movies with me, he got high in the carpark before we went in. I was so angry – why couldn't he just enjoy himself and my company without it? I felt so insulted. When we got home that night, he sat glued to the TV and I had never felt more

PARTIES, PILLS & PSYCHOSIS

unwanted or invisible before. I don't think he even noticed when I went to bed.

Tuesday March 30, 2010

I've been feeling weird about me and Dylan lately, not myself. A lot of it is to do with drugs – we took a lot of acid two weekends ago and it was a lot of fun. I laughed so much but all the other thoughts, the slight paranoia is coming back with anything now, although I'm not sure if it's just acid or all drugs for me. But I also know some part of it is normal because it's a drug and it's not always good – Dylan keeps saying that to me. But I'm getting off track, that's not even the point. It's Dylan, we're not a normal couple, we don't call each other just to chat, we don't go to the movies or the beach or go out to dinner. Originally I thought that was just us because we partied so much together but now I'm not so sure. I'm bored. This is the "real" part of the relationship, no exciting romance anymore. I'm bored with the routine of it all. I'm waiting around for something but there's nothing. It's only the next time we take drugs or get drunk. It's weird because I love doing that and I have fun and don't really want to stop but I want there to be something else. I don't want me and Dylan to fall into a rut. He doesn't make a big effort with me anymore. I feel like I'm trying way too hard to be perfect to keep him happy. It's just not me, I'm independent, I'm not clingy, I do what I feel like. I don't care what people think. When did it all change? Now I am thinking too much again.

Sunday April 4, 2010

We just spent Easter away, fishing, drinking and talking. I don't want to disregard what I wrote earlier but being with him, just me and him for a while, helped me get my confidence back with him. I think we're OK now. He smoked weed the entire time, though. It bugs me that he ALWAYS needs it. I think we are going to have another drug-free month now, which is probably a good thing.

CLARE KENYON

Monday April 12, 2010

I hate having my period, it makes me feel so depressed about my relationship with Dylan. Like yes I'm with another stoner who can't be bothered calling me, messaging me back, not seeing me during the week. It is really starting to bug me, the phone thing. I just don't feel this is really real anymore. I feel very patronised when he talks to me sometimes. I think I put us on a pedestal in the beginning really, which is why I feel so bad now. But I also know we're in the normal part, not honeymoon period etc., not calling me beautiful anymore, not needing to talk every day. Meh --I love him, he loves me, what else should I need?

Tuesday April 20, 2010

I feel like shit all the time now. I've tried to blame it on the drugs, on the fact we don't call each other much, the fact we don't have Wednesday night dinners together anymore, the fact that we're not in the "honeymoon period", I even blamed it on my period. But it's not that. How can I continually feel like this after I see him? It's him, I think. Because he's "hooked me in" he feels he doesn't have to try anymore. He is one of those boys who are romantic and sweet in the beginning but don't stay like that and, because I expect him to, I'm punishing myself and I think I'm screwing things up with him when it's not my fault. I haven't really changed, except my confidence with him is waning. After admitting this, I guess it's clear I haven't been happy for a while. I love what Dylan comes with – a group of friends, a lot of fun, new drug experiences, sex and intimacy. But now there's so many things about him that are getting to me and it's just that I'm so very much in love with him and can't get enough of him I haven't cared up until now. I just wish it was exciting again, and I'd get that warm fuzzy feeling again. Welcome to the boring everyday life of relationships, Clare. Also, maybe I'm used to being best friends with guys, telling each other everything. Hanging out with Jack today, it was just so easy with him and familiar. It always is, probably because we were so close. I wonder if it will ever be like that with Dylan.

PARTIES, PILLS & PSYCHOSIS

Friday April 23, 2010

I came home from Dylan's this morning bawling my eyes out. Last night while I was watching TV with Dylan and Joe and feeling like I was invisible, I realised I didn't really want to be with him anymore, which is so difficult to comprehend because I love him so much. But I think we both love the idea of it and not really our relationship, if we are being brutally honest. We're going to "talk" on Monday and I don't know whether to ask him to put in more effort or just end it because there's no point. Do we connect still or have we just run out of things to say to each other? Are we just in a rut? And we need to do something sober and exciting every now and again, get the endorphins/adrenalin – natural highs – going. Hmm ... as if that will change anything. Why is it so much easier to write than it is to speak? To be honest this relationship is bringing me down and it's not healthy. OK, yes it takes two to tango and I know I'm pointing all the blame at Dylan and so I'd be happy for him to talk to me and tell me how I'm different. Thinking about it, yeah I do think it will be over on Monday. God, how funny, from thinking he's the one to wanting to dump him. A lot can happen in nine months.

I gave him an ultimatum early on, which changed things temporarily. I basically asked him to figure out whether he thought I was worth the effort or not. If he decided I wasn't, then I wanted to just let him go. He took me out to dinner and apologised, promised he would change and that he wanted to be with me. He made me feel much better about us. But six months later it was exactly the same.

I was getting sick of his depressed unmotivated moods all the time, his laziness, when he stayed up smoking weed all night instead of coming to bed – even after I had had a horrible day and needed company. There were many times I wanted to break up with him and it was like my head was telling me one thing but my heart desperately wanted to stay with him and would hang on to all the reasons why I loved him, even though they started to be few and far between. He would get angry when I went out and partied with Lucy, told me I was a disrespectful girlfriend. He hated that I had kept in contact with Jayden. Dylan was unhappy in Perth and was thinking about moving to Jakarta around this time but he shut me out and wouldn't talk to me, so I had no idea and got angrier instead.

Drugs got us together, but it was also, I feel, what broke us up. I felt drugs and music were his first priorities and I was his last. He had enough of his full-time job towards mid-2010 and got a job at the local pub. By that time I had finished my TAFE course at the top of my class and was offered a junior consultancy job at a travel agency. The changes to our work-life meant I was busy during the week and he worked weekends when I was free. Our fights became more and more frequent and we were both getting sick of it.

There were a few standout things that made me decide to break up with him, one being when I went to Thailand on a work trip. I asked him to drive me to the airport the next morning. He said no because he was going to a friend's house that night and he would be hung-over in the morning. What a selfish person he had become, I thought. It made me so angry that for his girlfriend – someone he was supposed to love – he would not do a simple favour like this. I left for Thailand very angry and nothing had really changed when I got back. I was hoping he would surprise me at the airport but instead he actually forgot when I was coming home.

Also, in Thailand, one of the other travel agents on the trip had recently got married.

I asked her: "How did you know he was IT?"

She replied: "You just know."

And that made me realise I knew Dylan wasn't it and I now no longer wanted to be in a relationship I knew had no future, no matter how much I wanted him to change or how much I thought he might one day. Being overseas again made me remember how much I loved to travel, how I wanted to explore the world and be free, and so things kept adding to the growing list of reasons.

A big issue was the fact Dylan didn't like my friends. He told me this early on and I got quite angry because it seemed as if it was the

PARTIES, PILLS & PSYCHOSIS

fact they didn't get on drugs like he did. Or he couldn't smoke a bong with them or talk about music, as they weren't into dance music like I was. It was the year of 21st parties while I was with him and it bugged me he wouldn't come to any. My friends were my life and I wanted to share my life with him, especially when I spent so much time and effort with his friends. We had numerous fights about it, never coming to a compromise. And it made me feel like a nagging, controlling girlfriend, which I hated.

One weekend Dylan was playing an amazing gig, supporting a big international DJ. We had a fight beforehand when he told me he felt "obligated to do things for me". It was like a slap in the face. I left his house telling him I was getting ready for the gig but I had no intention of going and met my friends for a drink instead. I talked it over with Megan who was having similar issues with her boyfriend. The fight made me want to break up with Dylan there and then, call him up and ruin his gig -- I was so angry. But instead, because I really wanted to see the international, and being the supportive girlfriend I was, I got changed and went to the gig, but we hardly spoke to each other.

While we were watching him, Alex, one of his friends, said to me: "Clarreeee, you get to go home with the DeeJayy!"

It was like a flashback to a year earlier when I was happy and excited to be with him. It reminded me of why I had wanted to be with him so long ago, which had made me ignore his drug addiction, selfishness and the thoughtless things he would say. It was a glimpse back into the life I had been living – the DJ's girlfriend, the fun, the identity and the tag that went with that. I was addicted to that lifestyle, to the kick-ons, the free drugs, the gigs, the endless laughs, the fun people. I was suddenly over it and I couldn't care less that I was going home with him. It hardly made up for anything.

Saturday September 11, 2010

Another month of shit, disappointment and realisation – how did I fall for him? Well now I know after last night – a glimpse into the lifestyle of the DJ's girlfriend, the fun with that group, the dancing, the highness; that was the attraction, the pull. But every other day it's Dylan who hardly talks to me, selfish, lazy, making me feel constantly unappreciated. Wasting money! I know what I need to do but I just can't bring myself to do it. I don't want to be alone; it's been such a massive part of my life. But it's got to be better than feeling this low all the time ... or is this normal?

We had been text messaging each other "good night and love you" every night for over a year now, so when I stopped he noticed.

"So you are not saying goodnight anymore?"

"Well I can't act normal around you anymore when I don't feel right about us."

"Well you should say something instead of nothing."

"I have said something, a few times. Either you don't care or you're not listening."

And there was no reply, but he knew I was coming around at the weekend to pick up some Ritalin for Parklife festival. I told him I wanted to talk. I knew I was going to break up with him then, if he didn't do something drastic, but when I got to his house he had been up all night on gear with his roommate. I walked in and I could smell it, I could hear the thumping bass and I looked into his dilated pupils and at the sheepish grins on both their faces. I felt so upset and knew I couldn't stay for long before breaking down. I got the Ritalin and we walked outside. I looked at him pointedly but he didn't say anything; he stood there and gave me a hug. I drove off furious and upset. Why didn't he care about us anymore?

I sent him a message later that night and it grew heated. He belittled what I was feeling and told me I was "just emotional after a festival", which made me even angrier. He was drinking with his mates and didn't want to talk, so eventually he stopped replying.

Two days later we still hadn't spoken, so I asked him to meet me at work on my lunch break. I said I didn't want to drag it out any longer. We sat on a park bench, chain smoking, talking, crying, silent. Months earlier, Dylan had decided to move to Jakarta to live with his Dad, but

PARTIES, PILLS & PSYCHOSIS

until that eventuated we had agreed we would stay together and enjoy the time we had left. Now I had decided if he wouldn't change, then there was no point staying together.

He told me: "I can't give you any more than this", and so half-an-hour later we said an angry and sad goodbye; both our hearts were broken.

2011 - A WHIRLWIND YEAR

Sets On The Beach festival - March 2011

"Let's get this party started, Let's get drunk and freaky fly, you with me so it's alright, We're gonna stay up the whole night"
Justice – The Party

People were shocked and upset when our status changed on Facebook, particularly Dylan's friends, his Mum and his sister who I had become close to. They all said I was the best thing that had happened to Dylan, which made it hurt that much more. He wrote me a sweet email asking for forgiveness, telling me how much I meant to him and I deserved someone who could devote his time to me. I was upset for a long time and never understood the pain of a broken heart could hurt this badly.

I didn't like not knowing what he was up to and whether he was OK or not. A couple of months down the track, Joe got together with a girl called Zoe. She became the new "Redcliffe woman" and we quickly became close friends. She would often tell me how Dylan was doing and that he once said, "I was the one that got away". I was so angry at

PARTIES, PILLS & PSYCHOSIS

the unfairness of it all.

Thursday October 7, 2010

I hear a loud car – I wish it was him. I keep holding on to him but keep willing this feeling away. It's hard because I know I did the right thing but it just doesn't feel like that yet. I miss him, miss seeing "Dylan baby" come up on my phone. But I probably just miss the idea of him, of having someone – because I do remember a time when I felt just as awful as I do now when I was with him. I wish he would change, stop smoking weed. I wish he had said: "No Clare, I'd rather spend the rest of my time in Perth with you, rather than without you because that's all we have left", and it could go back to the time when it was "our weekends", not just his. But it happens only in the movies. You became selfish and assumed I would stick around after you finished your day shift and I'd sit with you while you were stoned or coming down playing video games. Then wait around and do it all again in 10 days. Then you send me this beautiful email saying, "I'm a special person". Well obviously not special enough for you to waste any time of your days off on. Not special enough for any attention from you.

The combination of losing my appetite because of a broken heart, getting off the contraceptive pill and taking dexies most weekends, resulted in me losing a lot of weight. Not that I was fat before, but now I was very slim and I looked and felt stunning. It was amazing for my confidence and just what I needed at a time I was feeling so low. The agency I was working at was very busy and I would never have time to eat, so that also contributed to my weight loss, I was now a size 6. I missed Dylan no end, but I knew I had made the right decision. If he wasn't willing to put in any effort for me, then what was the point? In his place I reconnected with my friends and remembered how amazing they were. Megan was going through a three-year relationship break-up at the same time, and then Lucy broke up with Ian, so we were all very supportive of each other and I spent more time with the rest of the gang to fill the void. I had been with Dylan for over a year, he had changed my life in good ways and bad and it was a strange adjustment to now be single again with a lot of free time on my hands. However, I had a distraction during the break-up that helped me to get through it.

Monday July 12, 2010

I haven't written about my business idea yet. It's big and ambitious but I believe I can do it and I want it so badly. It's so unbelievably perfect and it has huge potential. It is also my excuse to leave in a couple of years. Deep down I haven't changed, my goal to get away and be free will probably be forever, even though I have found ways to suppress it and forget. I love dreaming this dream. I must start working on it straightaway.

Earlier in the year I had come home to Dylan's house after a festival late at night and lay there next to him, thinking about the day, not able to sleep, as I was still pretty high.

"I just wish I could go to raves all the time," I thought, and from there an idea sprung to mind for a business. It was for a music festival tour operation in Europe, similar to Contiki but for music festivals, where I would take small groups of young people on a coach around Europe hitting up dance music festivals as well as big cities like London, Berlin, Prague and Amsterdam, organising festival accommodation and tickets, transport and hostel accommodation.

There were no companies marketing this to Australians, not even to Brits and other Europeans (well certainly not the kind of thing I had in mind), so I thought I was on to a winner. From there I started planning, researching, talking about it with people and developing the itinerary for my first tour while finishing my travel course at TAFE.

When I went to Thailand in September I went armed with my notes and drafts of tour ideas, and I spoke to the product manager of the tour group. We discussed things and he told me to "just go for it", and so I did. When I got home from Thailand I surged on with my plans and decided to move to London in order to pitch it to someone in the industry over there, as the business involved being in Europe. I asked Dylan to come with me and he said no as it was then that he was thinking about moving to Jakarta. We agreed it was silly to give up on our dreams just to stay together, but we promised to try to make it work for the nine months we had left together.

When Dylan and I broke up, my business became my obsession, my new love. I would race home from my job every night and sit at the computer working for several hours on it. I created a package to sell to people and promoted it on Facebook. I received an overwhelming response, people thought it was an amazing idea and said, "Why didn't anyone think of it before?"

This inspired me even more and I handed out flyers at festivals during the summer, posted ads on dance music forums and tried to get the word out as much as possible. My imagination was running wild, I knew in every bone in my body this was going to work, I would take people on an unbelievable tour, and it would grow into a huge company. My parents and friends were encouraging me to keep going and to follow my dreams. Everyone could see the brilliance in it and I believed anything was possible with the right amount of work and motivation.

But in January 2011, when I pitched the idea to my boss, a work colleague pointed out you needed a licence for what I was proposing. After further research, my heart sank, as it would cost around $15,000 and then upwards of that for public liability insurance. My dream was over in an instant and it was literally like my heart had been broken all over again. I had worked so damn hard on it, thought about it day in day out, spent SO much of my own money on it – I lost about $3500 buying early bird tickets to a festival, and advertising -- and it was all over in an instant. I posted it on Facebook and gave people their deposits back.

But I still didn't want to give up – the idea was too good to let go. I believed I could be like one of those entrepreneurs I saw at the many seminars Dad had taken me to. So from there I worked on a business plan, I went to the Small Business Development Corporation in the city and had a few meetings with advisers there. They gave me a template for a business plan, one that might be given to a bank when asking for a loan. The meetings I had encouraged me more and helped me with ideas on how to get it off the ground. I finished the business plan around April 2011 and by then I had also booked a holiday to Europe with Cory. This trip was going to be part-research and part-fun, in place of the tour I had tried to organise.

We were planning four nights in Berlin and four in Prague to party before hitting up Exit festival in Serbia, which was part of the itinerary I had created for the tour group. I was so eager to check out the Berlin nightlife because I hadn't done so last time. Afterwards, I was going to London on my own for a week to speak to some people about my idea. I had set up a meeting with a friend of a friend, who was high up in the travel industry and had started his own tour company. He was willing to meet me, read my plan and give me some pointers. Before I left, I also planned to pitch it to my boss at the new travel agency where I had begun working.

Sunday February 20, 2011

It's like I've reached this point, had this fleeting moment, a brief feeling this morning as I rolled up another five dexies for the next festival. I don't want to waste my time, energy and money with this anymore. I want to make something of myself. This is not as satisfying as it used to be ... partying. I wish I could find a way to make these tours work.

I was recruited to the new agency in March 2011 through Chloe, a girl I met in Thailand on my agency trip the year before. We became close and she convinced me to move offices as this one had all young girls around my age working there. The people I worked with at the other agency were older ladies and I wanted to make friends and enjoy myself more. So it turned out to be a great move. I got along amazingly with the girls who have now become very good friends. The owners of the agency were a young couple and I believed they would be interested in my idea.

At the end of 2010, Cory had returned from his big Europe trip; he had been backpacking for six months, much like I did. So we started to spend a lot of time together as he was living only about two minutes

PARTIES, PILLS & PSYCHOSIS

from my home and we now had so much in common. We talked about Europe all the time; he told me all about Exit festival and the Berlin clubs and I filled him in on what had happened with Dylan and me. We planned our European adventure and partied hard together that summer, as the majority of our friends like Lucy had grown out of it and didn't want to take drugs anymore. Lucy was focusing on her career and had moved in with her new boyfriend, Luke. More of my friends were starting to get concerned, especially Sarah, so we kept things even more of a secret. This possibly added to the fun – it was a secret thing between Cory and I.

Over the summer months of December and January, as I was building up the business and promoting it on Facebook, I met a guy called Anthony. I was at Barrick one night and he started talking to me after watching me shuffle. He was friendly and very cute, so I thought why not. We swapped numbers and he asked me on a date the following week. We went out for dinner and had a really lovely night. He was a miner from the east coast who had recently moved to Perth. He was tall, dark and handsome and had a great sense of humour. Above all, he treated me amazingly well and we didn't talk about drugs. In fact, he was almost the opposite of Dylan. Anthony was stunningly sweet and was not afraid to tell me how he was feeling, or the fact he was hopelessly shy because of how "amazing I was". I lapped it up, my heart had been broken and it meant so much to hear these nice things and that someone thought I was special.

After the date he had to fly away for work for two weeks, but he called me every day. In fact, he walked 500 metres up a hill every night to get a mobile phone connection and we would talk for hours. I liked him but I knew I was keeping him at arm's length. He asked whether we could be "official" but I didn't want to. I didn't want to be in a relationship again, I was going to Europe, possibly not coming home, plus I knew I wasn't over Dylan – it had been only a couple of months!

Deep down I hoped Dylan and I would get back together, that he would realise he couldn't live without me and would change, and for some reason not move to Jakarta. But when Anthony started to get serious about me and told me he was falling in love with me, I ran the other way and ended things with him. He just wasn't Dylan when it came down to it.

Wednesday December 22, 2010

I'm terrified and I'm over-thinking everything but I reckon I really do need to think about this one. I don't want to jump into something huge again; I don't want to allow myself to fall for Anthony. I don't want to go through all that heartache again if it doesn't work out. I thought Dylan was it and I was dead wrong. Anthony – what did you do to me in one week?! I don't want to hurt him ... is he just a rebound?

Sunday January 16, 2011

The past five weeks have been the best fun of my life. Festivals, music, great friends. Anthony is really amazing and so sweet. I'm not ready for this but I'm doing it anyway. I haven't let go of Dylan, can never stop thinking about him, sick of my stupid heart that is still attached to him. I want to move on. I'm pretending that's what I'm doing, but I wish I could be with him one more time like we were in the old days when we were in love and happy. Now I just feel guilty about Anthony because he is amazing and he took me to Melbourne to meet his family! What was I thinking?! I know in time I'll forget about Dylan.

On another note, I had to cancel my tour in July, probably a good thing but I am so disappointed. I always let my imagination run away with me. I need someone to be realistic for me and pull me back down to earth. I feel like such a failure. I thought I could prove everyone wrong and have a different life. But I am going to be normal and mundane living a 9-5 life like everyone else. How on earth could lil' Clarey think she could start a massive tour company?

As if. Stop dreaming.

PARTIES, PILLS & PSYCHOSIS

Monday February 14, 2011

Valentine's Day. I broke up with Anthony yesterday. It's too much, too hard and I don't want any of it. He's such a sweet guy but it's not what I want. I don't know if I was ever really into him or if I just told myself I was because I didn't want to be alone. I think he's a rebound and it's horrible to say but I really couldn't care if I don't see him again.

Tuesday February 22, 2011

My 22nd birthday night was last weekend. I love this day because it means my friends all come to Barrick with me, even though they hate the music. Lucy, Luke and I had lines of coke in the bathroom of the pub as a birthday celebration for me and I don't know how I stayed standing after all the tequila and jagerbombs[18]. I just want to record how awesome this night was, surrounded by all the beautiful people in my life. Thank you, universe, again for another amazing birthday. Nights like this just take all my stresses away.

I wanted to be single and free and focus on my business, but this was not on the cards for me. I met another guy, and yes, at Barrick again in April 2011, and he changed my life completely. His name was Josh. At that time I was going shuffling and dancing at Barrick virtually every weekend, so it was probably only a matter of time before I bumped into him. He was part of the "Barrick crew" and knew a lot of people in the scene. Even though I wanted to be single, there was something about him I couldn't say no to. In the first week we met, we went on a date every night and went away down south together on a whim that first weekend. I had been caught up in a whirlwind.

Josh was exciting to be around; he had an energy about him I was drawn to. He was incredibly sexy, funny, sweet, good looking and charming. He was in his late 20s, had a great job earning decent money and he lived in an inner city apartment with a view to the river. I felt sophisticated with him; we went out on expensive dinner dates and drank good wine. We fell for each other quickly and were caught up in the moment of being together. Work became our last priority, always rocking up late after spending the morning in bed together. Josh would call me three or four times a day just to say hi or tell me he missed me, and I would race home to see him every afternoon after work. After a while, I was basically living with him. He gave me a drawer to put my clothes in and I stayed over every night, but he never asked for rent as he used my car to get to work. It just worked better for us this way, plus we never wanted to be apart.

Tuesday May 3, 2011

I'm at war with myself, trying so hard not to fall for Josh, afraid I already have and still trying to enjoy it. It scares me so much how a guy can change my plans. There is something so seductively addictive about him, though – everything I've ever dreamed of. However, I don't feel so special around him. Sometimes yes, when he looks at me in that way and when he cuddles me so tight. But he talks about his ex-girlfriends like they're different pairs of jeans and I don't particularly want to be just one of them. I've gone against everything I've said to Anthony and to myself. I don't want to be in a relationship just for the sake of it, but here I am doing it. It's only been a few weeks but I've spent every night with him since we met. It's too late, I think I've already fallen for him and I'm walking around with this stupid grin on my face.

About a month into it Josh sat me down and told me he had something important to tell me.

"I want you to know this because it broke me and my last girlfriend up and I don't want it to happen to us," he said. "I have a four-year-old daughter."

Woaaah, I thought, and I took a big gulp of my wine before responding. I thanked him for his honesty and processed it when I got home. I realised, though, at that moment I didn't actually see a future with Josh. I just liked being with him for the now, in the moment. Dylan had left for Jakarta by then and I preferred having the company than being alone, didn't want the reminder of a broken heart. So I never let it bother me that much. Josh wasn't the kind of guy you marry anyway.

PARTIES, PILLS & PSYCHOSIS

Josh was a bad boy and I had a taste for them. But he was charming enough to make my friends and parents believe he was nothing but an angel. Lucy didn't like him from the start but I didn't even trust my best friend's intuition. We would take drugs together and party at Barrick till the early hours. I had bought a bottle of dexies off a friend before I met Josh and so I always had a supply when I wanted it. That, and ecstasy, had become my vice. I would take them at every festival during the summer season and most weekends. Dexies became like a security blanket when I went out; I didn't feel as confident if I didn't have them on me. We had coke occasionally as well; Josh had a dealer who would come round every couple of weeks; she was nice, too skinny and apparently had kids. They would sit together with a few of Josh's friends and smoke crack in the apartment, but it was something I didn't want to get involved in and stayed on the couch watching TV. I never said anything to him about my psychotic episode almost three years earlier; I had completely erased it in my mind.

I met his friends early on. There were two – Matt and Ricky – whom I got along with particularly well. Matt rented an apartment in the same block and would often have big parties. It was an attractive lifestyle these boys had – in their gorgeous, river view apartments with pools, spas, gyms and ping pong tables. It was so different to my experience with Dylan, in the broken-down, old party house that was trashed every weekend and smelt of weed and cigarettes. There, to an extent, you felt like a dodgy drug addict. Here it was classy, rich and everyone was smart and beautiful with decent corporate jobs. It was addictive and felt so normal.

Wednesday May 25, 2011

I'm crazy about Josh; it all happened so quickly. I don't really live at home anymore and a few days ago he told me he loved me. I said it back and I do. He's basically perfect; I don't want to mess this up. He has this amazing energy and constantly makes me laugh. Dylan is flying out to Jakarta tonight. I caught up with him yesterday and said goodbye. I am still sad about it, still wishing or thinking we could have something more. But the past is the past and I'm so happy at the moment with Josh.

Josh also sold drugs. I didn't know the extent of it at first, whether it stretched any further than the petty drug dealing common in the circles I had been around in for the past few years. But it came to a head when a fair amount of white powder known as R2D2[19] – kind of a mix between coke and ecstasy – popped up around his apartment. Because I had a lot of contacts I sent a text around to about ten people and some were interested. I was in a world where this was OK and everyone discussed it; it was stupid and dangerous via text and it would cause me trouble down the track. One night, I tried it when Cory and I got lucky.

I was out with Cory at Barrick while Josh was catching up with friends at another club. We went to get money out of the ATM and as I walked up I realised there was some money still in the slot. The guy in front of us was so wasted he didn't even pick it up. I grabbed it and passed it behind me to Cory, telling him to "get to the back now!" When I met him there afterwards, we counted it - $250!! Score!! We both knew what we wanted to do with it and I called Josh. We walked to get the keys off him and asked where the R2D2 was in the apartment and ran off giggling. But we couldn't find it. We searched and searched and searched. At one point, Cory went under the bed and found a bag of syringes. He held it up to me with raised eyebrows. Alarm bells started to ring – what the hell was this?

Eventually we found the powder and racked up a few lines. Ricky was home by now and we chatted with him for a while. My brother messaged me next and asked if he could buy some R2D2. I was so excited my brother was talking to me and said we would come round with it. During the 40-minute drive to his place, Cory and I, both off our heads, had a massive "deep and meaningful" about life, my brother and drugs. Cory was quickly becoming my closest friend and he understood me so well and I loved the connection I felt with him when we were on drugs together.

When we got there, my brother was so sweet and nice to me. I sold him a gram and hung out for a bit, then left to go home. I was so happy I had seen him again and he was being nice to me.

PARTIES, PILLS & PSYCHOSIS

When Cory and I got back to Josh's we had more lines and left the money on the table for him. Josh was home and had passed out on the living room floor. Cory and I watched the sun come up, looking out at the amazing view of the river. There we saw what looked like an organised run taking place. We laughed, watching all the fit, "normal" people running, while we were still high on a Sunday morning after being up all night.

Later, I questioned Josh about the syringes and he said they belonged to one of his friends. I didn't really know what to think. I ignored it. I guess love made me blind, yet again. Looking back, I just wasn't strong enough to make a big deal about it.

The months had flown by with Josh, and the departure date for my trip to Europe was getting closer. I wanted to talk to my boss about the business before I left, so I set up a meeting with her for the week before I was due to fly out. I was all prepared and very excited. I explained what it was all about, how it would work and I gave her my plan to read. She started discussing ideas with me, how we could get the other girls in the office involved as well. It was exactly what I had hoped for! She asked me more questions but I said everything was in the plan for her and to please read through it and to let me know what she thought. I came out of the meeting my heart pounding, hoping this was just the beginning for me and my business dreams.

Everything was perfect in my life except for a massive fight I had with Sarah. She had always taken a high moral stance and did not agree with my choice of lifestyle and always let me know about it; she had begun to get worried about associating with me because of her new career, and about my well-being, but she spoke to me about it an aggressive way. Sarah had spoken to Lucy about it earlier in the year and Lucy had then stopped taking drugs, plus she had begun studying. When Sarah found out I was still partying hard and about the text messages, she went crazy at me.

We had a huge fight and of course I defended my lifestyle. Then when she started attacking Josh, I defended him as well. She made me feel like scum, like an addict, when I knew it was nothing like that. I just liked to party, she didn't understand the world I was in. She had never been to Barrick or a drum n bass gig, hardly any raves. How would she know anything about it? But she was accusing me of all sorts of things and it really hurt. Sarah cut me out of her life and told me never to speak to her again while I was still associated with drugs. When I told Josh about it, he told me to forget about her. "Fuck her," he said.

The timing of that fight with Sarah was interesting, because the same thing had happened in the week before my first episode when I was nineteen. It was almost as if she could sense something was about to go wrong, that this time I was getting in way over my head.

The fight showed me later how detached I was from my life, from the "real world" – of drugs and crime; that how I was acting and what I was doing were really not OK. But I had grown up in a world where drugs were OK, from the very early days with my brother, to high school, and now in the music scene I loved. I didn't understand why she was so angry with me or why it was a problem. I felt I was like any other recreational drug user, no different to any of the well-adjusted people I had been hanging out with lately.

So I thought my life was more or less perfect, I felt like I was living a dream. I had a great job, was doing well in my career, I had a gorgeous boyfriend who loved me and a great group of friends. I had a holiday planned and amazing prospects for the future with my business goals. I thought to myself if London went well for me, that would be the end of partying and I would focus everything on making this business work. Europe came around quickly and my seemingly perfect world collapsed the weekend before I went away – all because of one damn party.

Wednesday June 22, 2011

I haven't written in ages because I haven't been at home! I've been living at Josh's for so long now, and it's wonderful. I love him so much I keep having to settle my heart when I see him and pinch myself to make sure I'm not in a dream as I sometimes can't believe someone as amazing as him loves me. I'm so lucky. Off to Europe in a couple of days, going to make my dreams come true! Josh

PARTIES, PILLS & PSYCHOSIS

supports everything I do and he cares so much about me. I am so excited, my future looks bright. I can't wait for Exit festival and to get to London. If things go well ... who knows what will happen.

THE BERLIN DAZE
JUNE 28 - JULY 2, 2011

"Those creatures arrive with a thirst they want quenched and as hard as I fight they still get in, to my head, to that watering hole in my head…"
Missy Higgins -- Watering Hole

Scribbling notes to myself in the Berlin hospital

PARTIES, PILLS & PSYCHOSIS

We threw a going-away party the weekend before we were due to fly out – just our friends at a bar and then we were heading to Barrick. Cory and I had a few dexies at the beginning of the night. We stayed drinking and catching up until around 10pm before heading back to Josh's apartment. I pranced around showing the girls his apartment, and the stunning view of the river and South Perth.

They gushed and giggled, "oh Clare, you are so lucky, this is so amazing."

I smiled and laughed with them ... "Yeah, it's pretty cool, hey."

We walked to Barrick and stayed all night. Unbeknown to me, Josh had organised an after-party at his house. By then, everyone but Cory had left. There were about 20 people at the kick-on. Josh knew some of them, but they were mostly random people. The music was cranking and everyone was drinking, dancing and playing ping-pong. Someone had brought out the R2D2 Cory and I had had a couple of weeks earlier and everyone had a line. Josh started to ignore me and was acting like a real asshole. Cory and I stayed together most of the night. We chatted to a few nice people but once they left we felt a bit out of place. The vibe at the party wasn't so good and the people, we agreed later, were not so friendly.

More drugs came out and I assumed it was the same as before. But it was stronger, much stronger, and I had a lot. My heart started to race, and my body felt overwhelmed with highness, euphoria, but it lasted only momentarily.

"Clare," Josh barked at me. "Come here!"

This was the first time he had spoken to me all night. For some reason I felt very shy; his eyes looked different, evil even. Paranoia had suddenly kicked in. The drugs overwhelmed me. I was breathing so heavily to try to calm my heartbeat down that I could hardly speak to him. I went out on to the balcony and tried to calm down, but my usual thought processes had changed. It was like something had switched in my brain. I suddenly blanked out emotionally as my mind started to race, and the tornado started to build up. I felt like everybody at the party was whispering behind my back. I had no idea where Cory was. I must have been standing still, staring into space scared for a while, as the next thing I knew Josh was leading me into his room where he sat me down in the walk-in closet, holding me.

"Clare," he said, "what's wrong?"

"What's wrong, Munchie?" he repeated, shaking me gently.

"I don't know," was all I could whisper back, because I didn't know, I didn't know if what my mind was telling me was real. I couldn't even look him in the eyes for very long. He looked at me strangely and made a spa bath for me, gave me half a Valium and my IPod.

Kissing me on my cheek, he said: "I'll be back in a bit, try to calm down."

I didn't realise how long I had been in there, but Josh came back and looked really angry.

"You have been there for ages, come on!" he said.

Maybe he was annoyed because I wasn't being an entertaining, hosting girlfriend. Perhaps that was how the drugs were affecting him, making him aggressive and angry. I did feel better by then and all I wanted to do was go out there and start partying again, have fun with these people, start drinking again. I went out again feeling more or less normal. A few people in the corner were having lines again, I don't know what came over me but I went and had another one.

After that I couldn't remember much – I think I faded in and out of the party. I remember at some stage shooting tequila, three or four shots, and everyone laughing. I remember we all went out to the park during the day to kick a football around and we watched as Cory stripped to his boxers and dived through a puddle. I remember I couldn't shake the anxiety at any stage but I kept trying to drink it away.

PARTIES, PILLS & PSYCHOSIS

The party died late on Sunday night – which meant we had been up on those intense drugs for 36 hours. I stayed at Josh's house, and I remember waking up next morning and freaking out about work and just having "The Fear" in general. But we went with the motions, like we always had, got ready, kissed each other goodbye and I started walking to work.

It was different this time, I couldn't shake the feeling someone was following me and I looked over my shoulder several times. I felt very jittery and anxious and I was turning the last two nights over and over again in my mind – what was real, what wasn't, what happened, what went wrong, am I getting sick again, do I need to go see someone at the hospital?

On the way I ran into Matt and his friend, and they offered me a lift to work. They were laughing and carrying on, saying how funny I was with the tequila and suddenly I was back there. I felt awkward and embarrassed around them, mumbled something and jumped out of the car. I could see Matt looking out of the window at me – a confused, weird look on his face.

It got worse when I arrived at work. I was taking in deep breaths but I couldn't stop my hands shaking or the anxiety that was welling up inside me. One of my bosses was there too; I couldn't let him know what I had been up to. My first phone call of the day came and the client started asking questions about her $20,000 Europe trip. I couldn't comprehend a word of it. "I-I'll call you back," I stuttered. I couldn't do this for another eight hours. I sent an imessage around to everyone: "Guys, I'm really sick, can I go home?"

My boss laughed and messaged back: "You're joking, right?"

Chloe came over to see me, took one look at me and she knew I wasn't OK.

"I'm so scattered, Chloe," I said.

She laughed knowingly, and said: "You should go home and get some sleep and come back later, hey."

So I grabbed my stuff, said goodbye and left. I felt suffocated in the office, but now I was out, what on earth was I supposed to do?

If my mind was racing like this after a big night I would take a sleeping pill and go back to sleep, and would always be fine afterwards. Usually it was just the after-effects of a big weekend and I had dealt with it many times before. All I wanted was to go home but I knew Mum would be there and I had to avoid her or she would find out what I had been up to. So I walked back to Josh's house, the only safe place I could think of, to plan my next move. I wondered briefly if I should go to the hospital and talk to someone there. Ricky was still at the apartment when I got back.

"You know he does this most weekends," Ricky warned me.

Was that supposed to scare me? I had survived a year at Club Redcliffe, but I realised Josh hardly knew anything about my past. I walked to the train station thinking about this.

Josh picked me up from the station but he was acting like a dick. I felt very awkward and intimidated around him. He didn't understand this and I didn't know how to explain it to him. He drove me home to get some Temazepan, forgetting Mum was actually at her salon. Then we drove back to his place. I should have stayed at home where I felt safe. Once at Josh's apartment, he tucked me in and left me.

Next morning I woke up and felt a little better or maybe I was just forcing myself to feel better – I was going to Europe today! Panic washed over me ... "holy shit, I still have to get to work to wrap up my bookings and PACK!"

I stayed at work for as long as I could, did a terrible job at leaving the girls notes on my bookings and hardly said goodbye. When I got home I realised half my clothes were at Josh's. I didn't know which backpack I would take, let alone what clothes. I started shoving things in my sister's bag, knowing my old comfortable Europe one, with its

PARTIES, PILLS & PSYCHOSIS

groovy patches, would be too big as I was going away for only three weeks this time.

I threw shoes and clothes and anything that was nearby into the bag, grabbed my passport and tickets and started packing my airport bag, basically with anything that didn't fit in my backpack. After half an hour I had to go or I would miss my flight.

Dad yelled at me on my way out: "You're going to the airport like this? What is wrong with you?"

"I'm fine," I yelled back.

"Make sure you go and say goodbye to Mum," he said and shut my car door, exasperated.

I rushed to Bunnings first to get a padlock and a few things, and paranoia washed over me when I entered the shop ... whispering and laughing, people were staring at me.

I quickly got out of there and yelled at myself: "Snap out of it, Clare."

I recognised these thoughts from last time but I felt I could talk myself out of it, as I knew it wasn't real. I knew I would be fine as time passed. I didn't want to admit anything was wrong because that meant admitting I had been on drugs all weekend and I would not be able to get to Europe, where all my plans and dreams lay.

I decided not to go and see Mum. She would recognise straightaway what was happening and get worried at the state I was in. I didn't want her to know I was taking drugs again. I drove quickly back to Josh's and realised I had left my phone there and there were heaps of messages and calls from Lucy and my friends saying goodbye and telling me to stay safe. I wish I had spoken to them, I felt Lucy would have straightened my head out, but it was just another thing that stressed me out at the time.

The last thing I needed to do was pick up my business plan ... and that meant going to see my boss. I called her on the way – she said she was home. I knew she was angry with me because of the way I had walked out on Monday but I would just have to deal with it.

Josh was driving us there and on the way Dad called ... "you forgot your passport, Clare."

I almost burst into tears. But I called Cory who lived around the corner from our house.

"Can you pick it up?" I pleaded with him.

He burst out laughing: "Yes, don't worry, we have time."

Then I realised I had read my itinerary wrong – take-off was still another couple of hours away. Some travel agent I was. I briefly relaxed but then we pulled up at my boss's house. I knocked on the door and Sonia did not look impressed when she opened it.

She handed me my business plan and said: "You were just hung over on Monday, weren't you?"

I nodded quickly, eager to get out of there.

"What did you think?" I asked motioning to the plan.

"It's good, we'll see how Europe goes first," she replied.

I didn't know if that was a good remark or not – did she think I was doomed to fail in London? But I needed to leave, so I said goodbye and hopped back in the car. "God dammit, Clare, why did you have to get so fucked up on the weekend, you are ruining this opportunity and now your boss thinks you're an idiot," I thought to myself. But soon we had pulled into the airport and I had to push it out of my mind.

Josh and I got beers while we waited for Cory. It was then I really started to freak out. I hadn't got my money sorted, my bags were in a mess, I hadn't put my phone to international roaming, hadn't booked

PARTIES, PILLS & PSYCHOSIS

a train to Berlin or our hostel for when we got there, or anything, and I STILL thought people in the airport were talking about me.

I tried to calm myself, thinking, "I would figure it all out later".

Cory and I had planned to wing it and go with the flow anyway. When Cory got there his smiling face relaxed me out momentarily. We checked in, but this eerie feeling of paranoia, with everyone staring at me and whispering about me, wouldn't go away. I just tried to ignore everything. Mum chose to call right then, and we had a fight on the phone.

"I'm fine, Mum, I swear," I said.

"Dad said you were in a complete mess when you left," she replied.

"Mum, it's OK," I insisted.

I don't know why I lied to her; all I knew was I desperately wanted to board that plane, escape from everything and get our adventure started. I didn't realise there was no escaping my mind when it sank into this weird delusional universe.

Once back at the bar, Josh noticed I still wasn't back to normal.

"When are you gonna switch back to earth, Munchie?" he joked, clicking his fingers at me.

I laughed: "I'll be right once I get there and get a good night's sleep."

Soon enough they were calling our plane. Josh hugged me for what felt like forever.

"I love you," he said, "I'll miss you and be safe," and turning to Cory, he said, "look after her."

I grinned. "Ha ha, I'm going to be fine," I thought. "Let's DOOOO this!"

And we walked through the gate, waving goodbye.

The plane ride was a bit of a mess. I hardly slept, thought I was getting messages through my headphones, felt famous like everyone knew a special person was on board. I hardly ate the meals, thought the movie was giving me messages and made Cory angry because I left him in transit in Bangkok (I couldn't even tell you why) and he almost missed the flight.

When we arrived in Frankfurt, it still hadn't passed. I realised I hadn't eaten in ages but got a drink instead as I thought food was "wrong". We went to catch the train to Berlin and I couldn't concentrate on anything, so Cory had to organise it all – and pay for it.

I knew I was really annoying Cory and he was tired too, so I just kept quiet until I felt I really needed to try to sort my head out and relax. We went to the bar and got a few beers. There we started talking about the party on Saturday night, as I really wanted to figure out what went on. I wanted to speak to him about what was going on in my head, as I trusted him, but he told me to "stop my depressing crap" and we didn't talk about it again. I couldn't just put it down to a bad party and intense drugs. I had started to think there were "messages" everywhere again.

When we arrived in Berlin, we were a little lost, but Cory got us to our hostel after a few subway stops he remembered from his previous trip. We couldn't check in yet as it was only mid-morning, so we left our bags and wandered off into town. It was a beautiful, sunny, hot day in Berlin and the atmosphere was vibrant. I remembered this place and how much I loved it. Adrenalin started to pump through me. I couldn't wait to hit the clubs. We wandered around Alexanderplatz for a while, one of Berlin's main squares. The place was heaving with people and it had such a cool vibe; young, hip people everywhere. I remembered why I loved Europe so much.

We went to a big music store that spilled over five levels. We were in heaven and spent a couple of hours there, wandering around listening to music and choosing CDs. Then we went to a little supermarket

PARTIES, PILLS & PSYCHOSIS

to get some things like shampoo and soap and wandered off to the park to chill for a bit. We sunbaked for a little bit but by then I just wanted to check in and shower because I was sweaty and dirty and felt uncomfortable. Cory wanted to stay there so I left him and said I'd meet him back at the hostel. I found my way back somehow from memory on the subway.

At the hostel, nothing the receptionist said about the rules went in. I grabbed my bag and walked up the eight flights of stairs to our 20-bed dorm. On arrival, there were some Australian guys half-sleeping in the room. They introduced themselves and we chatted about Berlin and the crazy warehouse clubs they had been at, like Watergate, which was close to our hostel. I went about getting myself sorted for a shower. I realised then how unorganised I was, all my stuff was in a mess. When I came out, Cory was back and we continued chatting to a few people in our dorm.

The hostel was huge, with heaps of people staying in it. It had writing all over the walls, like "if you haven't changed your clothes in a couple days, you know you've had a good time". There was a really funky, cool atmosphere and look about it. It was a party hostel with a big common room and already the people we met seemed awesome. But I thought I should be sensible and get a good night's sleep, rest my brain and body, and then I could head out with Cory the next night. So I lay on the bed for about half-an-hour listening to chill music before Cory came in and told me I was being "weak", which made me laugh. There was no excuse; we were in Berlin, the techno and clubbing capital of Europe. So after another 30 minutes, I joined Cory downstairs, outside, for our first drinks while we examined the Berlin map looking at where all the clubs were in relation to our hostel. The boys I had spoken to earlier were at a table about 20 metres away. I called out and asked what they were up to for the night. Soon enough we had joined them and started sharing travelling stories.

My paranoia and confused thinking came back and from there everything went downhill. I'm not sure why as I hadn't had any drugs then, but I thought everything they were saying was about me, and one of them kept looking at me. With a sane brain now, I can see this as being the fact that most people who have been travelling can relate to other people's travel stories and he was staring at me because he was trying to flirt with me. But I comprehended it all wrong.

The boys started to buy rounds of jagerbombs and vodka red bulls, so we were beginning to get very drunk. Eventually we went round the corner to get some food which I don't remember eating. We had some tequila shots, and then I don't remember the rest of the night, except the boy who looked after me after I threw up. I have some vague memories of being at a rustic, underground nightclub near the Berlin Wall with graffiti everywhere and thumping dubstep upstairs and techno downstairs.

When I woke up I had a massive panic attack. I desperately tried to get my head around the night -- I hardly remembered anything. Did anything else happen with that guy? How did I even get home? What happened last night? I had no idea where Cory was, he was still out and those boys had checked out.

I couldn't control my breathing and my heart felt like it was beating out of my chest. I thought I was going to die. I had a shower and sat down in it, letting the hot water soothe me back to calmness. My thoughts about the night before were in an irrational mess.

After my shower and I had calmed down, I didn't know what to do with myself. We had come to Berlin to party; I never thought for a moment what to do during the day, plus I had already done all the touristy things five years ago.

A group of Americans had checked into our dorm and I befriended them and agreed to go for a walk to the East Side Gallery with them. This is when it felt like I had floated outside my body and was looking down at what I was doing. I was acting really weird – I was eating food off these guys' plates and just wandering all over the place. If it wasn't so serious, it might've been funny.

I didn't feel like me, it was like someone else was controlling my movements and speech. I wasn't normal, I didn't feel normal and

PARTIES, PILLS & PSYCHOSIS

the boys clued into it pretty quickly and left me at the train station. I wandered around Berlin really out of it, I went through a supermarket buying a sort of cloak/shawl because I thought it was going to protect me once I got back to the hostel. Then I bought a packet of soup because it was liquid food and was "OK".

I went to a couple of food stalls near the train station where I bought a beer and listened to what was going on around me. I literally felt like I was in some whirlwind, or real-life tornado, people were looking at me, whispering about me; it seemed like they were all talking about me as I stood in the centre surrounded by food vans and tables. I was getting confused and I just didn't know what reality was anymore. I didn't know where I actually was.

Soon I heard some people speaking English – an American couple. I went over and said hi like I already knew them and they knew me. They said they were here to visit their son in hospital and they pointed down the train line. I wanted to go with them; I knew at that point I needed to go to hospital. I started to really panic for my Mum and she asked me later why I didn't go with them. I don't know, I guess I still half-thought I would go out clubbing that night and everything would be OK. I didn't think anyone could help me anyway, I didn't know how to ask for help. What would I say – "I'm thinking weird things"? Plus I hated hospitals, hated the memory of Alma Street and I didn't want to confess that I had been doing anything illegal. Then the couple left. But I took a mental note of where this train station was and tried to make my way back there a couple of days later, hoping to find the hospital.

When I made it back to the hostel, a creepy vibe had taken over the funky cool atmosphere from before. The place was really dark and damp and looked hostile and all the writing on the walls started to creep me out, like the words had been written to make me scared and make me feel like an idiot. I felt safer up in my dorm and Cory was there, finally.

Things become a blur after this. Each night before I was forcibly admitted to hospital, I would get drunk with everyone at the hostel, hoping it would get rid of my anxiety. But it meant I didn't remember anything next morning and it worsened my state of mind.

I know we partied hard again the second night and made some new friends – two Irish girls who were really lovely to me when I spoke about my concerns with Josh and that boy; they laughed at my paranoia as "The Fear" and there were no rules when you went travelling. But it was starting to feel like each night was a "test". I was getting more and more confused, and there were messages everywhere again.

I vaguely remember smoking weed with a Canadian boy and a few other times with some Spanish guys because I thought I was "supposed" to. I wasn't sure what day it was but I remember speaking to one of the hostel workers and told her I was having panic attacks. She told me to get medication and the two Irish girls walked around with me in the rain trying to find a chemist, but I had no idea what we were doing. I kept asking them about "messages and codes" and all the ambulance sirens and people outside were freaking me out. I thought I was going to be run over by a train.

I didn't have access to my phone as I didn't have international roaming, but I did have email and Facebook through WIFI so I could start contacting Josh. When I logged on, there were about five emails from him asking what was going on and if I was OK. I had received emails from my usual subscription contacts such as IntheMix, Beatport, and Moshguide as well, but I was convinced these were warning me and I comprehended them with a completely delusional mind. I can't begin to explain how far from reality I was at this point. One email entitled Monkey Business confirmed for me that I was acting like a complete lunatic. One travel email entitled "How's 2 rooms sound?' prompted me to go and move rooms in the hostel. A sale email from Myer saying "2 days to go" made me think that in two days I was going to die.

The hostel wireless password was hostel666 – which made me think I was entering a devil world each time I logged on and that everything was bugged. When I was logged on, something evil was hacking into my thoughts and my phone and broadcasting it to the world. I was clicking pages and pages again, like the first time I was sick, thinking there was some answer somewhere, maybe help even.

PARTIES, PILLS & PSYCHOSIS

Everything started to quicken up then, and I had a sense of urgency about the things I was doing and saying. After a while I could hardly speak, and everything came out as a jumbled mess, so I was even more convinced that email was the way everyone was communicating with me. The third night I was cut off from the bar and I think that's when Cory called the ambulance. I remember being in a different dorm now. I moved because I thought everyone in the upstairs dorm hated me, which was re-confirmed from the "coded" emails I thought they were sending me.

When I went to have a shower in the shared bathroom I couldn't wash myself because I had forgotten the soap, I couldn't change because I forgot my jeans, I couldn't blow dry my hair because I forgot the power adapter -- I was in a mess. Then I looked at myself in the mirror. My eyes were dilated, I looked gaunt, too skinny, I had dark circles under my eyes and I looked agitated, scattered, pale, like I had just seen a ghost. I looked into the mirror and said to myself, the last rational words before I was admitted: "If you don't sort your shit out, Clare, you are going to do something stupid like jump out of a building, you ARE going to die". And I could feel myself looking over to the window – we were about ten storeys high. My body trembled with fear as another panic attack came on and the tornado in my head built up all over again. I put my head in my hands, hiding my face, wishing I could get away from here and from my mind. I was so confused and scared, trapped in my thoughts. I didn't know whom to trust, what to do, or what to say. I was unreachable by another human being.

I must have been saying some trippy stuff and acting really weird. I remember throwing a trashcan in my dorm at about 3am because my head was hurting so much with thoughts and voices and craziness. I remember this because a Spanish girl came up to me and held on to me, saying "you cannot do this, please come with me", but I didn't follow her out. She must have gone to reception to tell them and then maybe that's when the ambulance came.

The ambulance officers tried to coax me into coming to the hospital. I thought they were all stoned and were just dressed up like this because they were taking me to a mad rave before we went to

Berghain. They smiled at me, like they knew I knew. I went with them and Cory came too. I smoked a cigarette in the ambulance and giggled; Cory couldn't help but laugh at me.

The officers left us in the waiting room, and I started to get confused – where was the party? From there I tried to convince Cory I was OK, tried to be normal. He was getting so angry with me, yelling at me, and when I tried to leave, he grabbed my jacket and pulled me down. This was exactly how it was with Mum in emergency three years ago, and suddenly I realised where I was.

When we went to see the doctor, she was holding a book with the title Schizophrenia. My eyes widened and I panicked, this was NOT me! But then I started to listen to Cory as he was describing my behaviour over the past couple of days and what drugs we had, Meow Meow, he said. WHAT!!?? I didn't know it was that! Alarm bells went off, I had heard about mephedrone and how bad it was. I was still stewing over that when the doctor asked me a couple of questions. No, I wasn't hearing any voices and I would be fine, I just needed some sleep was my answer. I shouldn't have lied but I had forgotten about my illness from three years ago and didn't understand the link between psychosis and schizophrenia. I was terrified of hospitals, plus I didn't want to admit anything in front of Cory, I felt embarrassed and stupid. The doctor said she would keep me in overnight, which I did not like the sound of. She assured me I could leave at any time.

In the morning, I got up and ran away, but I got lost and ended up in the basement of the hospital. I was wearing a hoodie (where did I get that from?) and short shorts and I smelt of cigarettes. I wandered through the halls, up and down this concrete place, thinking I was on some kind of journey and the signs meant certain things; green was good, go there, never go up, always go down. Thoughts were just whirling through my head.

Eventually I made it to some workers' rooms, where there were two men who looked at me strangely. One pointed upstairs and said "home", which is exactly where I should have been. He started tapping a phone and said "call call", so he connected my phone up and charged

PARTIES, PILLS & PSYCHOSIS

it, but I still had no international roaming and no German sim card, so I couldn't call anyone. He left me alone then and I found a door that led me outside. I was free! But I didn't know what to do now.

I wandered around and eventually found myself back at the hospital entrance where I saw Cory. His friendly face appeared out of nowhere and I felt myself grinning, returning to reality. He hugged me and said he had been looking for me for a while. He went to check with a doctor that I had been discharged as he didn't believe me, but I don't think they even had me on the list, so we left.

As we got farther away from the hospital, I started to get worried again. I remembered the past couple of nights and that I was going back to that horrible scary hostel. I couldn't decide whether to stay or go with Cory. If I went back, would I be trapped there? But what was I going to do back at the hostel? I knew deep down I wasn't OK, but I didn't know how to get help. Staying with my friend Cory felt safer, but a hospital is where sick people should go, right?

We were on the subway when I made a split-second decision and told Cory I was going back to the hospital. He let me go. But I couldn't find my way back. I was getting very lost on the Berlin underground network. Going back and forth, changing lines, going above ground to have a look around, going back underground on the subways for what could have been hours. Berlin is a huge city, with an enormous train system. I knew in the back of my mind where I wanted to go, though – the train station where that American couple had been because there was a hospital somewhere near there.

When I realised I had been doing this for ages with no ticket I panicked, as I felt sure a cop would get on and bust me. Plus I looked homeless, it was raining and I was wearing shorts and thongs. I hadn't brushed my hair or showered or cleaned my teeth. I eventually asked for help, or some people took pity on me. They were Italian boys from what I could remember. They asked me where I was staying and led me back there. I almost celebrated when I got back to the hostel just because it was somewhere familiar. I went up to my dorm, my stuff was everywhere, and there were beer bottles and food everywhere.

CLARE KENYON

What had I been doing for the past couple of days?

I think I went to sleep at some point because when I woke up it was night-time. Time to party! (Yes – I was that crazy! Because it was a "test" right?). I changed, which took me forever as I couldn't decide on anything, as I went back and forth to and from my bag. My head was hurting, my stomach hurt because I hadn't eaten in four days and I kept stressing. Facebook was messing me up as well. Going online was the worst thing for me during those few days – there were so many things that confused me more. I was certain everyone back home knew I had been tripping out for the past couple of days and making a complete fool of myself. Their statuses would relate to me and make me more afraid of everyone. I added my Mum as my "coded" way of screaming HELP to her. I couldn't ask for help normally because I couldn't even type anymore.

The bed above me was now occupied by a guy who was using his computer. I smiled at him and he said he had been to Berghain the previous night. The memory of what I was doing and what I thought I was going to do came back and messed me up again. He was sitting on his computer, probably talking to a friend back home on Facebook, laughing. But I was convinced – in fact, I KNEW he was talking through the devil wireless system to the people partying downstairs. They were all laughing at me. Because of this I didn't make it downstairs for a long time, although I tried. I walked down three flights, then back up two, and then down four and then up one. At one point I just sat down on the stairs but I couldn't cry – I had nothing left in me. My whole body was exhausted, my stomach felt like it was eating itself out. My mind was in so much pain. I needed water but was too scared to go and find any. I was too afraid to move even a little bit. I had forgotten how to look after myself. I wanted to get rid of this pain in my head and I gingerly looked out of the window. I was so high up and it was raining. Everything looked so bleak and scary outside. Ambulance and police alarms were wailing and the city outside was coming alive as night fell over the city. I wanted to jump out of the window and end this but I was completely paralyzed by my paranoia and I literally couldn't move.

I went back up to my dorm eventually, and that's when I realised my

PARTIES, PILLS & PSYCHOSIS

business plan had been stolen. I couldn't find it anywhere. I panicked, my heart and soul had gone into this, it was the only thing that felt real to me, and even though things were so messed up in Berlin I still had this lingering hope I would get to London.

This drove me downstairs in an instant where everyone was just chilling out, playing pool, and I sat down with three Brazilian guys because I knew they already knew me. Of course they didn't, and with their broken English it made me more confused. I went to get a beer and the guy on the bar looked so angrily at me.

"Not YOU," he barked, and I went away confused.

"What was that for?" I thought. I had no memory of being cut off.

I told the guys I was sitting with that someone had stolen my plan; they told me to tell the hostel workers. It was at that point I realised two hostel workers were sitting at the next table, their eyes darting nervously to me every couple of seconds. I went up and said someone had stolen the plan but they must have thought I was a raving lunatic, because of course no one had stolen it – my stuff was just scattered everywhere in my room.

At that moment, Cory came in and dragged me away. We sat down in a different room for a while, not saying anything. But the tornado in my head came back, everything started to whirl around … thoughts, codes, messages, emails, what people had said, laughter, the angry look on the bartender's face. My mind felt like it was going to explode, the pressure was so intense. Something from deep within my subconscious was building up, and then out of nowhere voices were echoing around me, telling me everyone hated me and I should do something about it, shouldn't put up with it any longer, and it all became too much. I hated everyone, I wanted to hurt someone and beat the crap out of them. The voices were getting angrier and I felt aggression rise up through my body. I got up and punched a guy who was standing nearby with a group of people.

Next thing I knew, there were hostel workers around me, protecting me or protecting everyone else, I wasn't sure. I could hear the 30 or so people in the room had moved outside to the smoking area and were talking loudly and laughing. I started to get up. "Fuck everyone," I said. I was going to end this. But someone slammed me back in the chair. I felt like I was SUPPOSED to jump off a building, though. Didn't they all want me to? I was angry they had tried to stop me. It felt like someone else was controlling my brain and making me do things, telling me that's what I was supposed to do. Then four cops rocked up – three men and a lady. They were so tall, like giants. I instantly felt afraid. I could hear the hostel workers and Cory explaining what had been going on, but they had got it all wrong! It wasn't my fault! I started to speak up.

"No, they drugged me! They stole my stuff! Don't you know who I AM," I yelled out.

And at that moment – it was probably the mention of drugs – the lady cop twisted my arms around behind me, handcuffed me, shoved my head down and walked me outside to the big cop car, more like a truck. She strapped me into a straitjacket and I tried to fight it. Cory had followed with my bags and sat with his back to me, his head in his hands.

"Fuck you, Cory," I said, as I knew this was all a conspiracy against me.

The last thing I remember was being handcuffed starfish style to a bed in a hospital where an Australian doctor was talking to me. He called me Rachel. I was so scared by that point and I think I started crying. Maybe I was Rachel now; maybe I was a completely different person. I had no idea who Clare was anymore. But then I got angry again and started swearing and wrestling with the constraints, knowing this wasn't right and I hadn't done anything wrong, some other high power was controlling me still. I yelled out at them. It was all so scary and I didn't know what was going to happen. The handcuffs hurt my wrists and I felt so uncomfortable spread out, so vulnerable and small. And then I started crying again. The doctor kept trying to talk to me but nothing he said was registering. I started to think of Mum and Dad.

PARTIES, PILLS & PSYCHOSIS

"Please don't tell them," I begged. I thought I could sort myself out, but I had no idea I was about to be committed in a locked ward. The doctor promised not to say anything and said he couldn't without my written permission. He shoved a pink pill down my throat and Cory still had his back to me, hadn't looked at me or said a word the whole time.

The next morning I woke up in a concrete hell.

BERLIN AND THE CLARE I'VE NEVER MET BEFORE

"There's a monster in my head, there's an animal screaming that I'm on my neck, no no you better get off my friend, what a mess we're in, no no you better run my friend"
Boy and Bear – Milk and Sticks

by Cory

When Clare asked me to write about our time travelling in Berlin I must admit I was scared. Did I really want to revisit those crazy few weeks, which almost didn't seem real? But by writing about and revisiting this time, as hard as it has been, it has also felt like a cleansing process and one that was necessary for both Clare and I.

It all started the weekend before we left for our big adventure overseas. I guess we were both feeling anxious and excited about our travels, deciding to have a big bender of a weekend before we left. Clare was dating a guy at the time, and after a few lines and dancing at a nightclub, we decided to head back to his house to continue the party. This was the day before our flight, and looking back on things, it was a very bad idea. Things began to get out of hand and Clare and I were taking too many drugs. I guess, like most young people, we thought we were invincible. Sunday morning became Sunday night and I headed home to pack my suitcase and try to get some sleep.

Next day Clare phoned me to say she was already on her way to the airport but had forgotten her passport. When I dropped by her family's house to pick it up, I remember speaking to Clare's younger

PARTIES, PILLS & PSYCHOSIS

sister and telling her I would take good care of Clare.

I guess things went wrong from the beginning of our flight. We were in Bangkok and about to board the plane for Frankfurt when we decided to go to the toilet quickly. I told Clare I would meet her at the front of the female toilet. Time passed as I waited for her and I was becoming increasingly anxious. Where was she? Our flight was about to leave!

An airline official told me I had to get on immediately and I ran as fast as I could. When I got on board, I saw Clare in her seat just staring blankly ahead. I was furious! Why would she get on the plane without me and why hadn't she just waited outside the toilet? We didn't speak much on the plane but I let the anger go and we arrived in Frankfurt excited and ready to make our way to Berlin.

We boarded a train and spent the next few hours hopping on and off various connecting trains. I constantly needed to make sure Clare stayed close to me, as she kept drifting off to have a smoke or to try and grab some food. Didn't she realise we didn't have time? I didn't want to miss any of our connecting trains.

When we arrived in Berlin, we started to unwind and after dropping our bags off at the hostel, we headed to the park to sunbake and enjoy the nice weather. Clare wanted to go back to the hostel earlier than me, which reminded me why I enjoyed travelling by myself. As much as I enjoyed Clare's company, I also enjoy my own solitude and acting independently.

We decided to meet back at the hostel later. Although Clare had a bit of trouble getting back to the hostel, she had a map and when we eventually did meet up everything seemed fine. We met some people from Sydney at the hostel and spent the night drinking with them. Clare probably had too much tequila and, after having a quick vomit, she headed back to the hostel with one of the guys. Things were getting odder and odder, and I decided it would be a good idea to hit the clubs and get my mind off them.

CLARE KENYON

Over the next few days Clare and I became more and more distant. She told me she wanted to go to Prague straightaway and I kept telling her we would, after the weekend. She was really starting to annoy me; she seemed like a different person and was acting like a child at times. She had trouble sleeping and gave me a haunting stare whenever we were together. She was becoming rude and hostile, with most of the problems occurring at night-time. She would put her music on really loud, even though people were trying to sleep.

At one stage, after I had almost fallen asleep, I was disturbed by Clare rummaging through my bag. I kept telling her she needed to get some sleep and that everything would be fine. My patience was beginning to run out. I remember going out to get lunch, to find Clare outside the hostel with her backpack on, ready to head to Prague. Things were becoming more and more weird, and I didn't understand why she was being so irrational. What could I do? I was in the middle of a foreign city with someone who was acting completely differently from the person I knew.

After going out by myself on Friday night, I woke up to several texts from a new friend at the hostel who was concerned Clare was becoming irrational. But I kept telling myself everything would be OK. After speaking to the girls at the hostel, we decided it was best that Clare and I go to the hospital and see if there was any way they could help. We got in a taxi and Clare become hostile, at times trying to open the door. As we got out, I dragged her into the hospital and tried to get some help. The language barrier with the person at reception was frustrating, and as I tried to explain what was going on, Clare took off and ran away. I felt so helpless and frustrated. Why didn't she want to get help and why wouldn't she admit something was wrong?

I eventually found her around the hospital and we spoke to a local, who was willing to take us to another hospital. Clare was going in and out of her normal state and we almost got hit by a train while crossing the road. My feelings of despair and stress could have reached breaking point there and then, but I managed to calm myself down and took Clare back to the hostel and bought some sleeping pills.

PARTIES, PILLS & PSYCHOSIS

I was tired and so frustrated with Clare at this point and I started shouting at her. Looking back at how helpless I felt, I can only imagine how helpless and scared she must have felt too. I told her she needed to get some rest and we definitely weren't going out that night. A few hours later she came down to the hostel bar and drank with everyone. She was convinced we were going out. Eventually she went back upstairs and after talking to people who worked at the hostel, we decided something definitely needed to be done. The ambulance was called and we managed to convince Clare to get in. The most frustrating thing at this point was the fact I couldn't just take Clare to a psychiatric hospital – she needed to want to go.

We arrived at the hospital and were told to wait until a doctor was available. I had to forcefully pin Clare down in her seat so she would not escape. For what felt like hours, we sat in the waiting room, Clare crying and screaming while I tried to hold her.

When the doctor came and spoke to us, I learned about Clare's previous psychosis condition. I knew she had had problems in the past, but why had she not told me it was psychosis? After some discussion, she was put in a room for voluntary patients for the night. I felt relieved and headed back to the hostel at around 3am.

Next morning, I went back to visit Clare. At reception I asked what room she was in and was told she had left. Where was she? Not only was there a language barrier, but also I had no idea where she was. I almost broke down crying. I walked around the hospital grounds to look for her and found her sitting there smiling and listening to her IPod. She seemed dazed and confused. I asked her why she wasn't in her room and she said she was free to leave. I was sceptical but when I spoke to the receptionist again, she confirmed this was the case. I felt frustrated to hear this and I had this sinking feeling of helplessness.

As Clare and I walked outside, one minute she would be like her old self and next minute she would start acting oddly. I lost all patience with her and after an argument, I told her to go back to the hospital and I would visit her later. A few hours later as I was about to leave the hostel, Clare showed up. I can't begin to express how frustrated and annoyed I felt. I had just gone on Wikipedia and looked up psychosis. Why wasn't anything being done to help Clare, and what else could I do?

She kept telling me she felt better and the doctor had given her medicine, but I felt even more sceptical. She went to her dorm and a few hours later I went to see her. She was putting her high heels on!

"What are you doing?" I said. "You need to get some rest, you've been cut off from the bar and you are not well."

Clare gave me a really chilling stare and said: "You would like it if I jumped out of the window, wouldn't you?"

I felt sick to my stomach. There was no way of communicating with her at this point. She was becoming aggressive, and when she headed back down to the bar she started lashing out at the people around her. I convinced the staff to call the police and an ambulance, and I remember one of them telling me I needed to stay strong for Clare.

The police and the ambulance arrived and Clare was put into a restraint. Seeing her in such a state was distressing, to say the least. When we arrived back at the hospital I spoke to another doctor. This was the first time I felt the anxiety, stress and helplessness lessen somewhat. Despite Clare's protestations, I gave the doctor her parents' phone number and was told she would now be in an involuntary ward for at least a few weeks. As sad as it was to leave her there, it was good to be reassured she would now be in good care. As I caught a taxi home, I felt a sense of relief.

The first few visits to see her, during the next week, were rough; she looked so out of it and at times could hardly open her eyes due to the medication. The hospital staff were helpful, though, and the other patients seemed to become less and less scary or different as each day passed.

I managed to speak to the Australian embassy and Clare's mother, which helped to ease the burden. Clare started to appear more stable

PARTIES, PILLS & PSYCHOSIS

and eventually we were able to start having a conversation. I knew I couldn't take her home but I was happy to stay in Berlin and keep visiting her. There was no way I was going to leave her there by herself. I will be forever grateful to the people I met in Berlin during this time, including the staff at the hospital and the hostel for helping me keep my spirits up. After that first week, I began to feel like I was on holiday again, and I hoped this positivity helped Clare in her recovery.

Visiting Clare wasn't a burden, although I did feel guilty I was enjoying the sights of Berlin while she was locked in a ward. I realised, though, it was important to be strong and positive for Clare, especially when I visited her. The hospital was in a nice location along the river in Kreuzberg, and it was good to take her outside a couple of times so she could also enjoy the beauty of Berlin in summer. Another pleasant moment was when I went to the CD shop and bought Clare some new music and a CD player so that, in a way, she could enjoy the music scene of Berlin that I was embracing.

Eventually Clare's mother, Serena, flew in to take her home and I can't begin to imagine how she would have felt. But it was good to know Clare was about to leave the hospital and head back to Perth to continue her recovery.

When I see Clare now it is hard to believe this incident in Berlin even happened. She is such a strong and remarkable human being and a great friend and I know if anything happened to me, she would be there for me. She is someone I hold close to my heart, and I think we both learned so much about ourselves during the time in Berlin. I hope she doesn't regret her past too much or be too hard on herself, because everyone makes mistakes. She never ruined my trip and I don't hold anything against her. I can't wait to see what the future brings for Clare. Life is precious and so are the special friends we make along the way.

Cory xx

THE HOSPITALS

Credit - Joseph Henson Photography

"There's a sadness on your face, you're like a motherless child who's longing for comfort, what's running through your veins that's causing you such pain, does it have something to do with the pills they gave you?"
City and Color – O Sister

I didn't know what was going on when I woke up in Berlin next morning. I had only vague memories of what happened the night before. But it smelled like a hospital and it felt like one too. I could hear someone wailing and footsteps nearby. I was in a room all by myself, it was big and I could see the windows were locked shut. It was a bright sunny day outside.

I got out of bed and saw my backpack on the floor. I gingerly walked out and saw an exit door. I ran over to open it, but it was locked. I was in a locked ward. The ward, or really the corridor, was about 30 metres long, with rooms either side, and a smoking room and a dining area down one end. Maybe 30 patients were there. Nobody spoke fluent English. There were two young girls lying on beds in the corridors; they had tattoos and piercings and multi-coloured hair. They smiled at me and said "Guten Tag." Then one started crying and the other one went to comfort her. I went back to my room and cried myself to sleep; I didn't know what to do or who to speak to. I was so scared and all alone, plus the tornado in my head hadn't gone away.

That night I woke up and when I fully understood I was trapped in the ward, I locked myself in a bathroom. I sat under the shower, fully clothed and cried, I don't know how long for, maybe an hour. The girls from the night before were banging on the door, yelling at me to open it. They thought I was slicing my wrists with their razor. To be honest I was eyeing it off. Eventually, the nurses had to break down the door to get inside. They couldn't hear me from outside, so they probably did think I had killed myself.

After that they realised they had to keep an eye on me. I spoke to a couple of doctors but I was too afraid to say much, and my words came out as mumbled, confused, incoherent sentences anyway. I didn't trust anyone. Cory must have found my passport and given it to the nurses because eventually they found my name and I gave them permission to call my family as I didn't know what else to do. That call in the middle of the night must have been the scariest, worst-ever thing for my parents.

Once I had spoken to Mum and Josh the tornado in my head started to calm down. Mum can explain things to me in a way that makes sense.

"You're sick," she said over and over again. "Don't you remember the last time?"

I really had to sit there and think about this because I didn't remember; I had blocked it out, it didn't exist anymore because I had continued partying with drugs for almost three years and was fine. But there were so many similarities – I was back in that confusing hell again, whether I liked it or not.

I wasn't allowed to go outside, not even for a walk or some fresh air. I would sit at the window in the dining room and look out at the families in the park wishing I could be there and feeling the sun's rays.

CLARE KENYON

My only contact with the outside world was Cory; he stayed in Berlin and visited me almost every day. The nurses allowed him to take me outside once but I was still paranoid, thinking people were whispering about me. Thankfully, he bought me cigarettes and CDs, as smoking was the only thing to do in hospital – apart from listening to music, eating the crappy food and going silently more insane.

There was a tiny smoking room inside the ward and there were maybe one or two therapy classes for the two and half weeks I was there and they were in German. Some patients could speak some English and we tried to make conversation, but I thought they were all there for me and were telling me things in codes; it was still all a conspiracy. I knew I was crazy when I looked around and saw the other patients in the ward. I didn't think there was any going back, I knew this was real and I was going to be like this permanently, marked as "insane" forever. This started to bring me down, way down to a whole other depth of emotion I had to endure.

I didn't get along with any of the nurses and doctors except one. I annoyed them at the start because I had an obsession with the computer; I fought them to go on it, as I believed there was some message inside that I had to read. I also sent incoherent, panicked emails to Josh and Mum. They were giving me medication in the morning and at night, as I was anxious all the time. Then this was increased to midday as well.

At one point I didn't think I would be able to go home as all the patients in the ward were given letters from the hospital that stated the date they could leave. Mine said sometime in September, which was wrong as Mum was supposed to be flying over to pick me up on July 17. That sent me into a spin and I called Mum who said everything was OK and she was definitely coming. They wouldn't allow me to leave the hospital of my own accord until I was "better". I had to have a chaperone.

From: Clare Kenyon (clarekenyon@hotmail.com)
Sent: Thursday, 7 July 2011 9:40:48 PM
To: Mum

PARTIES, PILLS & PSYCHOSIS

Subject: no im not ok I am stuck in a pshc ward thy think im going to kill someone of something
As IF!!!! They are pumped full of drugs I don't understand. I just want to be back home with you but they have all my passports safe just saw the link on Facebook with Cory it is FREAKING SCARED in here.

From: Clare Kenyon (clarekenyon@hotmail.com)
Sent: Saturday, 9 July 2011 8:03:27 PM
To: Mum
Am trying to work out a wa< so so you don't have to come, I'm spending a lot of money here 0 me and Cory will go to London. This place is making, me worse

From: Clare Kenyon (clarekenyon@hotmail.com)
Sent: Saturday, 9 July 2011 8:00:20 PM
To: CORY
Subject: WE MUST GET OUR SHIT OGETHER AND FLY TO LONDON IM PAYING: THIS HOSPITAL IS CONFUSING ME AND MAKING ME WORSE; SWEAT ON MY LIFE:
PLEASE COME SEE ME THIS ARVO WIHT TOILETRIES AND WE CAN GET A PLAN TOGHETER ONLY 195 EURO TO GET TO LONDON:

PLEASE BELIEVE ME
CLAREY

From: Clare Kenyon (clarekenyon@hotmail.com)
Sent: Saturday, 9 July 2011 7:56:47 PM
To: Josh.
Subject: Hey baby can U transfer that $1500 so I can get the fucke out of here!!!!!!!!!! LOVE LOVE LOVEXXXXXXXXXXXXXX

Hi Babe

I have been in contact with your Mum and sister. I know what's going on for you at the moment. I'm so sorry to think what a terrible place you must be in right now. I'm so concerned for you but I know you're in good hands and whatever treatment and help you're receiving is completely for your own health and wellbeing. You need to just go with the flow and know that everyone here loves you and wants you to get better as quickly as possible. You are in my thoughts constantly, Munchie. I don't think transferring that money is going to make any difference to your situation at the moment since you are in total care. But don't worry it will be here when you do actually need it.

Your doctor has my details and hopefully he'll call me soon and we will have a chance to speak! I am absolutely dying to hear your voice ... I beg you to please just let them help you, baby. The doctors know what is best for you right now, even though it might not seem that way. I miss and love you, babe, and I want you home and well asap.

Just in case you get an opportunity to call me yourself my numbers are 0410 703 678 and 9325 6579. Stay in touch if you can... Love you. Josh xxx

From: Serena Kenyon (serenaxxxxxxxxxxxx)
Sent: Thursday, 7 July 2011 11:29:15 PM
To: Clare Kenyon (clarekenyon@hotmail.com)
Hello darling girl,

Sending you lots of love from Dad and me and Christopher and Char. We all want you to get better so you can come home. You are safe where you are and you must stay there until you are well enough to come home. I know it's difficult, Clare, and you don't really understand at the moment, but this is how it was in the early days of treatment in Fremantle. You are sick again and you need to concentrate on getting better. We're speaking with Dr Gandor. We love you so much. Just "be" where you are at the moment and let the doctors and nurses help you. Much love. Mum xx

So it just became a waiting game, waiting for Mum to come and rescue me so I could return to my reality. There were a lot of young patients in the ward, around my age, but I didn't know German and

PARTIES, PILLS & PSYCHOSIS

they hardly knew English, so I found an English book and read that most days – managing only one page every fifteen minutes or so. At other times I listened to my iPod or had really long showers, hoping to wash the dirt away that I felt like on the inside.

There were two ladies in my room who could speak some English and they translated the letter from the hospital authorities and gave me subway cookies or magazines when they went outside on visits. They told me to "be brave" and would pat me on the back when I was upset. There was one chubby boy who was interesting– he would ramble on and on, and it seemed the only English he knew was "They are telling me from space, they will come for you and me, I'm Harry Potter, do you know Harry Potter, powers are mine".

Finally the day came when Mum was due to arrive. The one nurse I got along with came in and gave me a high five.

"You made it, Kenyon," he said.

He made me laugh, relief washed over me. I burst into tears when Mum walked through the door and I hugged her for a long, long time. I showed her around the ward and the nurses let me outside. I basked in the sunlight and breathed in the fresh air. Mum and I walked along the river where I tried to explain what happened. Although I felt safer with her, it didn't seem completely "normal" yet. It seemed as if people were still whispering and conspiring against me.

When we got back to the hospital I said goodbye to the nurses and thanked them, and the chubby boy gave me a big hug and wrote down his name, making me promise to add him on Facebook. When I looked him up, his name didn't exist.

Mum and I stayed in a hotel that night and Mum bought Cory dinner to say thank you for saving her daughter's life, because that is exactly what he had done. In fact, if he hadn't directed the hostel owners to call the police, I think I would have definitely jumped off something or tried to hurt myself – anything just to stop the voices and forces in my head hurting my soul anymore.

I spoke to Josh and Dad that night and shakily posted on Facebook that I was coming home early, which in hindsight wasn't the best thing to do. But I still half-thought everyone back home knew everything anyway; after all, they had been posting all these things that weekend about me...

We got up early next day and flew to London where we connected with our flight to Bangkok, and from there to Perth. The plane was awful, Mum was getting annoyed with me because I was saying weird things and keeping her awake; I couldn't concentrate on a movie and I was constantly moving about. But the reality was the "tornado" was back. I was in a confined space in this plane, surrounded by people, and the memory of the flight to Frankfurt was coming back. I felt like everyone could hear my thoughts and was laughing behind my back.

"Look at this loser, she had to get her Mum to pick her up" ... I just couldn't stop thoughts like this racing round and round in my head.

It was a relief when we finally landed in Perth and Josh came to pick us up. I was so happy to see him; he brought me one of his jumpers and I wrapped myself up in it and let him hold me and kiss me and care about me once again. He made me feel normal again, made me feel like ME. I had lost all notion of who I was, but Josh loved ME and that meant something.

Back home at Mum and Dad's, we lay on my bed and I explained, again, what happened. We also went through what happened at the party before I left and tried to make sense of it. Basically, we agreed I was an idiot for having more lines. When he said goodbye to go back to work, he made me promise to do exactly what my parents wanted and what the doctors said, not what I wanted. I must have given the impression to people I was fine now, because I was home, and I could go on living again and everything was sorted. But this was only the beginning...

That night my brother called and yelled at me on the phone.

"Are you OK?" was his first question.

PARTIES, PILLS & PSYCHOSIS

"Yeah, I think so."

"What did you have?"

"I'm not sure, Meow Meow, I think, and weed."

"What the hell is wrong with you, Clare? Why are you doing that shit, you idiot?"

I couldn't say anything back.

"Well now you know drugs are not for you, so stay away from them, OK?"

"Umm yep ... bye."

And I hung up, feeling so much worse.

I got aggressive with Mum again that night and tried to fight her, she tried to take my phone and computer away from me, which was a very good idea, as it was what tripped me out last time, but I was 22 years old now – Mum couldn't control me anymore!

When I went to bed I cried and cried, as I was starting to comprehend what I had done, the money it had cost to save me, what Mum had gone through and I apologised over and over again. Mum gave me a valerian to calm me down and in the morning we went straight back to Alma Street – a place I swore I would never go back to.

Alma Street was more or less the same the second time around – same halls, same constricting walls, same rooms, and same depressing vibe. And that smell – the kind of smell that seeped into your body and spoke of anxiety. You fall asleep to it, you wake up to it, and it's always there in your clothes. The smell of sickness and hopelessness – it was everywhere. It reminded me of Charlotte's time, it reminded me of my last time, and awful memories continued to flood back during my stay there.

It took all day to get me admitted into a bed again, sitting in the waiting room. Meantime my boss was messaging me, telling me she understood and I could come back to work whenever I was ready. I was paranoid again and remember sitting at lunch with Mum in a café in Fremantle thinking the staff were all laughing at me and I hid behind a newspaper pretending to read it. But then the words in the newspaper started to scare me too and I asked Mum if we could leave. I couldn't rationalise anything, it was all so real still in my head.

I started to get scared as the hours went by, waiting and waiting, and I started to remember where I was going. Once inside the ward, everything looked depressing. It was dinnertime and I could see the patients hunched over their trays, slowly spooning soup into their mouths. It was quiet, oh so quiet, and morbid, and there was a dim light over everything making it seem even gloomier. I didn't want Mum to leave, I didn't want to be alone again, alone with my festering thoughts. I felt like a young child clinging to its mother. As soon as she left, I asked the nurses for some sleeping pills. Some nurses from last time were still there, including Rex, who remembered me.

"You were so set last time, Clare, you promised, what happened?" Rex said.

I shrugged him off. "You don't know me," I said to myself. "How would you know what it's like out there?"

I saw a lady wandering around whom I recognised from the previous time, either she had been there for three years or had been readmitted. Her name was Barney – I'm not sure what her illness actually was but she moped around the halls day in day out dragging her feet. Seeing her again added to the sadness and hopelessness I felt about being back in this place.

On the first morning, I tentatively walked out of my room to breakfast. I grabbed my tray (oh it was all coming back to me, the awful food). I sat down with some people who were a lot older than me. I was listening to only parts of their conversation.

PARTIES, PILLS & PSYCHOSIS

"...they all thought I was crazy, I stayed here a week."

"I have a type of schizophrenia where I still know what's going on."

"I have depression."

"Depression," said another like he was ticking off a list.

I looked around the dining room behind me; there was a fat lady, a man shaking, a man whispering to himself, and a lady staring off into the distance. I wanted to curl up in a ball and die. I felt so disconnected from everything, myself, my family, and reality.

Am I like these people? They looked at me, expecting a story. I started to struggle with my words and my hands started to shake, and I mumbled something incoherent. I felt like a complete retard. What was wrong with me? I was speaking to Josh fine just yesterday. They looked at me in pity, and left and I went back to my room and cried until my nurse came to see me.

We walked off to one of the TV rooms and sat down. Her name was Fiona, and I liked her straightaway. She was a Mum and started chatting about her kids. I started to cry again when I thought of my Mum and what I had done to her yet again. She rubbed my back and said everything would be OK. And then I opened my mouth to speak but nothing came out; my brain just couldn't function.

"I can't do anything. What is wrong with me? I feel like a retard," I got out finally as I looked down at my hands and fingers that were angled in weird ways.

I clenched and unclenched them. I am crazy, I thought miserably.

"Oh honey, you're just jetlagged, your brain hasn't caught up with your body yet," Fiona said.

She made me feel better, but that afternoon the doctor had ordered brain scans.

CLARE KENYON

"They think I'm a retard as well, I have ruined my brain for good," I thought.

They were scary, strapping my body down and my head wrapped up. I wondered as my head went through the scans if they could see how awful I felt. Was there a whole section of my brain gone now? Do I not have common sense anymore, conversational skills? Have I lost my ability to be witty, flirty, fun? What have these drugs done to me? Because it was my second episode it was protocol to scan my brain and especially after they learned what drugs I had taken. Thankfully I hadn't done any permanent damage and it was just jetlag. But it started making me think more seriously this time.

After a couple more nights' sleep, I settled in a bit more as my brain started to reconnect with my body. My friends came to see me at night during visiting hours and I explained to them as best I could what had happened. I had had a lot of time to piece together those final days in Berlin before the cops came but to this day it still isn't clear. I was really in a different paranoid world. Cara, Tahlia, Megan, Ana and Rachel, who had never been involved with drugs, were especially worried. We had a few funny moments when my friends came to see me, and we have a laugh about them now. I don't remember much of it because I was a bit of a space cadet but my friends have filled me in. We were eating pizza when Barney kept coming up to hug my friends. When she started to hug Aiden - the most reserved of our group - he started to freak out. Barney just wouldn't let go and Aiden didn't know what to do. The look on his face was priceless. The nurses had to forcefully drag Barney away from him.

In terms of my paranoia, nothing had changed, and in fact after a week it got worse. Most days I was sending trippy messages to my parents who had no idea what to make of them. Basically I was just scared and didn't trust my nurses to tell them anything. I was pacing back and forth in my room for hours as the tornado built up and up in my head, but I was too scared to go outside. I couldn't read books or listen to the radio or do anything as it would make things worse.

When I first arrived at Alma Street, the nurses had taken me off the medication which had been given to me in Germany and only just started to work. They thought the dose was too high. But I deteriorated as the days wore on. Once Mum kicked up a stink, they realised it was a bad move and after a few sessions with my psychiatrist he put me back on a low dose and told me whenever I felt or thought something, I should talk to a nurse. So I did ... when I thought the TV was sending me messages, when the patients freaked me out, when I heard a voice speaking to me, when I thought someone was speaking about me through the radio. And each time I did this, they kept feeding me more and more medication.

As well as my morning and night pills of Risperidone and Quetiapine whenever I was really bad during the day, they gave me tabs of Olanzapine that dissolved instantly and calmed paranoia and anxiety in one go. My medication doses kept increasing and increasing. After another week of this I was an emotionless zombie. I didn't know if I was actually depressed anymore because I couldn't feel anything except numbness.

Slowly my paranoia subsided, my psychiatrist told me to "challenge it", think to myself "was this really real?" They told me I was lucky because I had what they called "insight" to my illness and could recognise my symptoms, which was true – I now remembered everything from last time.

After a while I wasn't complaining of any voices or the TV and radio "speaking to me" and I stopped telling people I was going to kill myself so the nurses began to trust me, and I was able to go home some nights. But home didn't feel like home anymore. I had been living at Josh's for a couple of months so I didn't know these people, didn't understand my family anymore, didn't recognise my room. I walked around, looking at photos of me and my friends, wondering who that girl was. She seemed so far away now. Inside the house Mum and Dad muted the TV and turned off the radio because they knew I would think the voices on there were talking about me. Plus whenever I said anything it was virtually in a whisper. I felt very uncomfortable.

After my mind had settled, I started to become closer to the other patients as they told me their stories. One very beautiful and smart lady with two kids was homeless. She put herself in hospital because she could feel her symptoms again. She was a dexamphetamine addict and had developed psychosis from it. Alarm bells were ringing, as I had taken dexies all the time. Once, when I stood in the middle of the ward, waiting for medication, feeling like chaos was all around me, she said: "Just keep telling yourself, Clare, it will be over soon, it's not real." She knew exactly what my mind was going through, and I will never forget it.

There was a personal trainer who had been in for about a month. He had depression, but he walked around smiling all the time. He told me he had put on a mask every day of his life and he didn't know how else to be. Again I could relate to that from my younger life.

There was a Dad who also had depression but was not making any recovery whatsoever. He was really sad to talk to.

I often smoked cigarettes with a bipolar hippy who told me she was a junkie and her parents had given up on her years ago. Her friend brought her to hospital because she was screaming that bugs were crawling all over her. Her vices were weed and heroin.

There was another homeless junkie who told me his Dad kicked him out when he was younger because he was partying so much. All their stories were so sad, and I just couldn't believe how lucky I was to have the family I did and who hadn't abandoned me in Berlin.

An ice addict was admitted one night, and we definitely knew all about it. She came in yelling and swearing, fighting the nurses and just being a horrible bitch. She was skinny, with sores all over her face and rashes all over her body. We called her the reptile. I saw her next morning in the breakfast room; she was shaking all over and had a deadpan look in her eyes. A woman who looked like her Mum was brushing her hair.

The following day she came outside with us for a smoke and tried to talk to us, but all she could say was, "yeah what a fucking cunt", or

PARTIES, PILLS & PSYCHOSIS

"fuck yeah", or "fuck that, "cunt this" or "cunt that". She was repulsive and scary, but clearly so very sick. The nurses would point her out in conversation and say things like that's what you could end up like if you stay on drugs. I had never felt so low in my life – that was what I was being compared with.

There were some interesting patients, too, this time around. There was gorgeous, rambling old Betty. She was chubby, with dark hair and a funny laugh. She would talk all the time, even when not spoken to. She would ramble on and on about her old life "back in the 60s", her old sweethearts, her old hobbies. I'm sure she thought she was helping, and she did, but she told the same story over and over again, as though she had forgotten she had said it ten minutes earlier. She made me think she was lucky to have lived as long as she had so she could tell a story. Many times she would say to me, "tell your story, Clare".

Then there was Mary and Frances whom I called the Zombies. They never said anything but just moped around the halls with emotionless expressions. They would sink in their seats staring out of the windows all day. I saw a light flicker in Frances once when her husband came to visit; she smiled a few times and said a couple of words.

At this stage, my parents were becoming quite angry about the way I was being treated at Alma Street. At the outset, there had been the matter of my medication being screwed up and now they felt they were shut out in relation to my recovery.

As I got better, I spent more time chatting and smoking with other patients. We would talk about the nurses, probably because there was nothing else to do except whinge. I learned about their experiences and discovered they were being treated badly too.

Because so many sick people were coming in every weekend, the majority being psychosis or depression-related, they would kick some out before they were well again. I relayed this to my parents and they decided they would move me to a private hospital. So they more or less demanded I should be discharged. I discussed this with my psychiatrist and arrangements were made for a transfer the following week.

It was interesting to discover down the track an investigation had been launched to determine why so many people were committing suicide after they had been discharged. Some psychiatrists had quit and a report was written in 2012 about the terrible state of WA's mental health system. In 2015, an inquest began into the number of Alma Street Centre patients who took their own lives.

Before moving hospitals I stayed at home on the weekend and I had a huge fight with Mum, which was kind of pivotal in my recovery, kind of what I like to think as "my brain switching back".

During the week, Dad had put on his investigative journalist hat and called all my friends to ask them what was going on. He and Mum had thought the Berlin incident had been caused by a one-off slip-up at a party; they weren't aware I had been doing drugs since my first stint in hospital.

Dad asked everyone and most of them kept as much as they could from him in order to protect me. But one friend, Melissa, told him everything – all about Josh, about me selling drugs, about us doing them and about my time with Dylan. And Mum blew up; she sent a message to Josh calling him a bastard. I was with Lucy and Megan at the time when Josh called me.

He was so angry on the phone, calling my friends and my mother four-letter words I don't want to repeat. I tried to tell him to stop but I was virtually at a whisper. It was registering very slowly what had happened and I told him I would call him back once I had sorted it out.

After hanging up I got angry with Mum via a text message.

"What are you doing speaking to Josh like that?" I demanded.

"We will talk at home, Clare," she responded.

Lucy tried to calm me down before she and Megan dropped me

PARTIES, PILLS & PSYCHOSIS

home, but I had a huge fight with Mum. She was crying and yelling at me.

"How dare you lie to me and treat us like that," she said.

I yelled back as I defended myself and Josh, telling her I felt like attacking her, and if I hadn't been so drugged up, I would have. I don't know why, I felt angry and I hated her but it was like someone was still controlling me and I was SUPPOSED to hurt her. I was in two minds, one where I was still trying to defend my lifestyle and the other where all I wanted to do was hug her and say I'm sorry, I knew I was in the wrong.

"Over my dead body will I ever let you go back to the lifestyle that threatened your life," she said.

It silenced the room. I froze. Her words stinging me. I had never seen her so angry with me before. I didn't know what I was supposed to do, I was angry at Mum for reacting like that and Melissa for being a snitch and I was upset by how Josh was going about everything. But really, deep down, I think I blew up because I knew now it was all over. Everything was out in the open, my parents knew about me taking drugs, and it felt like I was a fourteen-year-old again, not allowed to go to that party, not getting my own way.

After the fight, Mum dropped me back at Alma Street and left me alone for two days to fester. It was probably the abandonment that I needed.

On Monday, Fiona, my nurse, asked me what had happened at the weekend. After I told her, she said I had to make a decision – I could shun my parents, move out of home if I wanted, nothing was really in my way, I was 22 now, an adult, and independent from them.

"Who are the most important people in your life, Clare?" Fiona said.

Tears were rolling down my cheeks as I replied.

"My family."

"Boys come and go, Clare, but your family is forever," Fiona said.

She told me to think about what Mum would be going through right now.

"Think about what you have done as a teenager and a young adult and what do you think she's doing?" she said. "She is blaming herself."

I started to sob uncontrollably and she held me until I calmed down.

"You're at a point in your life, Clare, where you need to make a choice, you could turn out like that girl with the rashes or you could have kids yourself and live a successful life. You do want to get married, don't you?"

I never thought for a second that my lifestyle would prevent me from getting married and having children. I had always had a boy in my life. But she was referring to a permanent mental illness, such as schizophrenia, and what that could mean for my future.

I didn't have to think for too long, I knew I wanted to be healthy above all else, and I texted my parents to let them know. Mum leaving me alone made me realise what it would be like to have no contact with my family and I didn't want that. I knew I needed her help if I wanted to recover. I figured I would have to do whatever it took to get my parents' trust back and that meant going to do a course in cognitive behaviour therapy at the private hospital.

This place was like a hotel; my room was beautiful, I had an en suite bathroom and a TV. There was a chef who cooked gourmet meals and the nurses were all lovely, so different to Alma Street. I felt really positive when I settled in. But instead of a sick patient, they treated me like a dirty drug addict. The nurses would stand and watch me while I peed into a cup every morning just to reassure themselves I hadn't snuck out during the night to get drugs.

PARTIES, PILLS & PSYCHOSIS

It was the most degrading part about it. I wasn't the sexy, cool party girl anymore here. I found out the nurses were like this because most of the people there my age were drug addicts. But these people challenged my perception of who an 'addict' was. Most were educated, had typical middle-class jobs, friends and families who visited often and they seemed to celebrate their party lifestyle. In Alma Street there was a sense of hopelessness everywhere; many people were without much support and often homeless.

When I went out for a smoke on my second day, I met a few of the patients and sat listening to their conversations. They had been in hospital together for a while. They were laughing about the parties they had been to, the stupid things they had done and all the good times. It made me laugh as I remembered my own good times, instead of looking at everything in my life as one huge horrible mistake.

When I told them my story, and that I was arrested overseas, I made the cut and I fitted in with them. I had "quite the story", they said, and they taught me the hand-signal druggies in the hospital would use to acknowledge each other in the hallways, as they said "Mentaaall" instead of hello. It was a celebration of who they were and they thought it was cool. I joined in but I felt stupid, I did not want this to be my life, I didn't think it was cool anymore. I didn't think my story was cool at all. Every time I laughed a little I would remember what my parents had been through to get me home, what Cory had been through and I would stop in an instant.

Later I thought that maybe the patients were doing this because they didn't have much else in their lives, they were really sick, stuck in their ways, and had been in and out of hospital several times so why blame them for enjoying themselves as much as they could? But I intended to be different and I didn't sit with them much after that.

One boy, in particular, took an interest in me. His name was Jed, he was an accountant and meth addict. He was very cute and funny and asked if we could hang out, but I so did not want to invest any time into a boy, especially not this kind. I had started to realise my choice in boyfriends had not helped my situation at all. Plus I hadn't officially broken up with Josh yet. My parents and my doctor were putting pressure on me to do exactly that, once they found out about the drugs at his apartment. Everything came out during that weekend I had stayed at home. I told my parents basically everything through fits of tears. I felt so much guilt and shame I just wanted it out of me.

In hospital, it became apparent to me what kind of guy Josh really was. I thought about the way he had treated me after the fight with Mum, the way he spoke about my family and friends, about him telling my friends he would not be giving up drugs and this was "Clare's problem, not his". He thought he was doing the right thing by saying it was either drugs or him, but really he wanted to wipe his hands clean of my drama. I realised I didn't actually know him as well as I thought. Things started to become awkward between us, I stopped answering his calls and his texts and I didn't let him come to see me at the new hospital. I was sinking into myself.

Eventually I sent him a text message as my confidence was completely shattered and I told him I had to be away from any influence and give up on that life if I wanted to stay well. He called after the message and we talked about it for a while. He said: "If Melissa hadn't said anything, we would have made it through together."

I didn't know how I felt about that; I didn't think it was the right answer at all. I knew now what Melissa did was the right thing, and she did it to help me. When I was honest with myself, I wanted Josh out of my life. I couldn't invest any more emotional energy in him and the relationship. I had to focus on myself. I was confused about how I felt about him anyway, I wasn't sure if I liked him as a person anymore, I wasn't sure if I had ever loved him or if it was just an infatuation. Through my time in hospital, I saw him as arrogant and rude and a complete jerk when he was supposed to be a loving, caring and supportive boyfriend. I started to remember things, like how he had a few lines before meeting my parents at dinner for the first time, the drug dealing and the syringes under his bed. But at the same time I knew this whole other sweet side to him before all this had happened. In the end I put my trust in my Dad who begged me to realise Josh was not a good person.

PARTIES, PILLS & PSYCHOSIS

My psychiatrist was a cool guy, he seemed to get me, he seemed to get all the young patients in the hospital and would laugh about getting high with us. Not that he condoned it, but he wanted to relate to us so we could be open and honest with him. At first he asked about my drug use and he was writing a long list, plus my record showed "girl punched person in hostel and was straitjacketed to hospital", so he didn't exactly have a good first impression of me. He put me in drug and alcohol addiction therapy groups, despite my protests. And I sat there for a week, fairly confused, surrounded by junkies and depressed alcoholics fighting their cravings. They were all confessing their issues, their weaknesses and their troubles. It was an intensely emotional time listening to it all and meantime all I was thinking was "hell I just wanted to party".

The group therapist wanted the patients to speak up, but when he asked me things, all I could say was "look, I don't think I should be here". And of course what does that sound like? Denial!

However, they got me to go through it. "Do you need something when you go out, do you feel weird if you don't?"

I said I definitely preferred to be out on something but I never physically craved anything. The patients would look at me sadly.

The nurses told me later that putting me in addiction therapy was a scare tactic, and it really worked. I identified with almost all the patients. I reasoned I could easily have ended up there for longer if I didn't change my ways. I knew I had an addictive personality or I would have stopped the first time. Not necessarily a substance addiction, even though that could have come somewhere down the line, but an addiction to partying and the fun lifestyle. Now it was right there in my face, the results of a party life, and I couldn't ignore it any longer.

At the end of that first week, I became an outpatient attending cognitive behaviour therapy. This was a group therapy course over two weeks for eight hours a day. My sister had done it when she had anorexia and it had made a huge difference to her. There were five other patients – Rose, an ex-army officer; Julie, a retiree; Matt, who was middle-aged and unemployed and lived with his Mum; Sarah, who was bipolar and unemployed; and Ness, an Irish housewife.

On the first day we told each other our stories. They all had depression and some had very sad stories. I hadn't been officially diagnosed with depression yet but when we did a quiz on what we thought of ourselves and I gave myself 0 for everything, the therapists assured me I was in the right place.

The course was very intense and a real eye-opener for me, especially in relation to what I thought of myself and why, plus how others viewed me. It taught us to identify our core beliefs, things that had been ingrained into us when we were young. For me, they included things like I was a loser and a stupid, try-hard bitch (where have I heard that before?).

I realised the years of bullying from my brother had done significant damage to my self-esteem and I had been on a constant quest to prove myself to him and to others around me I wasn't a loser and this had turned into a tiring and unhealthy pursuit.

When we went around the circle discussing things, the common theme was everyone wanted to be liked, wanted to fit in, wanted to find somewhere they belonged – this from a range of people battling depression and self-esteem issues. It was sad to hear and so easy to relate to.

It was hard listening to what the therapists thought of me – that I was shy, quiet, kept to myself, agreed with everyone, couldn't stand up for myself. But I'm thankful now as I have worked on these things and have become better for it.

We learned you had to change the things you think in order to change the way you feel and I use this practice every day now. I learned what it means to be assertive and it is a skill you need to acquire in order to communicate effectively with people. Therapy taught me I had been a "passive" person my entire life and as such I had devalued my feelings by never speaking up.

PARTIES, PILLS & PSYCHOSIS

It also taught me that because I had been overly helpful all my life, this meant that deep down I felt I didn't matter or had low self-esteem. It was great to realise this wasn't the case and that it was OK to stand up for myself.

I perked up slightly by the end of the course. I had huge support from the other five patients, with whom I'd become quite close, and they would tell me I would be "just fine" and "I'm so young". But it was easy to believe you were OK in a safe hospital environment. On the outside, however, where you had to face reality, it was so different.

After two months in various hospitals I was ready to come home, but not after a strong lecture from my psychiatrist. He explained this had been building up in my brain for a while and because I had had the symptoms for so long it really was imperative I never did drugs again as the likelihood of it happening all over again and then developing into schizophrenia was huge, because this was my second episode. This was also when I found out one of Mum's cousins had schizophrenia, which terrified me to the very core. I hadn't known it was in the family.

Also, my doctor made me fess up that, over the years, I had been ignoring many psychotic symptoms. At the time, I associated psychosis only with weed, not with amphetamines, uppers or party drugs. So I ignored any symptoms, thinking it was "just the side-effects of the drugs", not an illness. The fact it had been building up over time and especially in the months before Berlin made sense because my life had become erratic again; it had a crazy sense of urgency about it, and I was becoming disorganised. At the time I thought it was just because of Josh's energy and because I was half-living out of home, but I recognised this was also what had occurred the first time I had become ill.

The following week I started work. It was so good to see the girls again, I had missed them and they were so supportive. My boss was very good about what had happened and I was so lucky I hadn't been fired, considering how irresponsible I had been before I left for Berlin. I wanted to get stuck into work and focus on my career, but it just became a reminder of what I had lost, that I had thrown away my

CLARE KENYON

business dream just to get high one night. And so I began to sink way, way down.

MUM'S STORY

by Serena Kenyon

The phone wouldn't stop ringing. Thinking it must be time to get up, I stumbled into the kitchen and answered it.

"Hello, Serena speaking."

"Mrs. Kenyon? This is Dr Gandor from the Vivantes Hospital in Berlin. Your daughter Clare is very sick but she is safe, she's had a psychotic breakdown."

I looked up at the clock, it was 2.30am.

Twelve days later – Friday, July 15 – I was on a plane to Berlin via London. After many hours flying and many more sitting around in airports, without any sleep, I was a bit of a wreck. During the trip I tried to imagine what would confront me at the hospital and how I would handle it.

Interspersed with this attempt at orderly thought were feelings of such intense sadness I would burst into tears – much to the embarrassment and concern of the passengers sitting next to me.

And scattered through those feelings was a sense of "well, here we go again, Clare".

And the memory of all the events three years ago came flooding back. How could we be doing this again? Oh my God, how could things have screwed up so badly - again? What haven't I seen, what have I missed, why didn't I see this coming? Blame, blame, blame. It has never left me – really – and now it was firing up all over again.

So how DID it get to this point?

Clare had been working at a travel agency as a travel consultant. She didn't enjoy it all that much, but it was a job and she was hell-bent on doing some more travel. Her father and I were hoping the job and lousy pay would bore her sufficiently to motivate her into returning to university.

She and Lucy were seeing a lot of each other and spending all their weekends at "duff duff" music festivals and gigs. I cannot understand what attracts people to this music – to my ears it is loud, artificial, head-banging, repetitious and utterly tedious. In my opinion, there is nothing pleasant, melodic or soothing about it. But each to their own – my dislike of it was never going to alter the fact that Clare did like it.

But what I didn't understand was the drug culture that pervaded this type of music. Didn't understand, didn't know, and didn't think -- it just never crossed my mind. So which rock had I been sleeping under?

I was also sufficiently naïve and trusting to assume that Clare's first episode of psychosis, her stint in Alma Street and the long recovery had scared her sufficiently to never touch drugs again. I assumed she had taken on-board what the doctors and social workers had told her, and she had been so sick she would never want to repeat the experience.

It had certainly scared me to blithering idiot status, but apparently not so Clare.

PARTIES, PILLS & PSYCHOSIS

So Clare, Lucy and Cory and a few others were always at "duff duff" events. Out all night and at weekends and sleeping it off during the day seemed to be the routine. I just couldn't relate to it at all and I saw it as a horribly unhealthy, unnatural existence.

Then she met Josh and life took a turn for the worse. I thought he was the ultimate in sleaze; a complete asshole and I didn't like him at all. Clare's Dad, Adrian, and I met him on a couple of occasions, but essentially he was kept a well-hidden secret from us (probably because we didn't approve). Clare was besotted.

Clare was becoming very messy and disorganised, always "rushing" and very forgetful. She was becoming very slim, bordering on thin, but she looked very beautiful, which did wonders for her self-esteem after the horrible weight-gaining side-effects of the anti-psychotic drugs. But I should have started to recognise the signs. Instead, I saw her happy and confident again, seemingly enjoying life, and I have to say I felt some relief and tried to feel OK about Josh.

Clare had come up with an idea for a travel-based business – a very good idea I have to say. She researched it well and spent hours writing up a very professional business plan. She was hoping the owners of her travel agency would support her venture.

She was very determined and decided to travel to Europe to a couple of festivals to research her idea, then on to the UK to meet the nephew of one of her Dad's friends who had expressed an interest in helping to finance the venture.

It sounded quite promising and exciting. Clare was very positive and enthusiastic – in fact, we hadn't seen her like this since the time she was planning her trip to Europe with Jack.

But then things started going even more awry. We saw less and less of Clare as she "moved in" with Josh into his apartment in the city. She would come home to pick up or drop off clothes and bits and pieces with a bit of a "hi Mum" along the way. Her car resembled a charity shop jumble sale after the shoppers had ransacked it – complete mayhem and chaos. Her room was worse. The "floordrobe" had reached knee-height and the contents were most likely life-threatening to anyone who ventured inside the door.

She seemed terribly rushed and scatty, evasive and defensive and over-the-top-happy in a frenzied sort of way. Phone calls and text messages seemed to be my main communication tools with her as she was so "not around and non-conversational".

I had no idea what she was doing, but whatever was going on I didn't like it. It sounded way too phony for me. Josh worked part-time. How could he afford a luxury apartment in the city? Clare never answered any of my questions. She said she was very happy, life was great, she was focused on her business plans ... so "give it a rest, Mum, and be happy for me, please".

I tried. But as the date of her departure drew nearer, her father and I became increasingly concerned about how disorganised she appeared to be. Tickets/accommodation/itinerary/packing – none of it was happening. She was just partying on and rushing around in ever decreasing circles achieving nothing.

She was due to fly out on Tuesday June 28 and the last time I saw her was the previous Thursday because I was busy at the salon and she didn't come home. I kept ringing, she promised to call in and see me: it never happened.

I didn't know there was a party happening at Josh's place over the weekend before she was due to leave. In fact, I didn't know what was happening at all. I kept on ringing and asking about the chaos in her room and her preparations, but was constantly told "it's OK, Mum, it's OK, I'll get it sorted", or words to that effect.

Clare didn't come home on the Monday night before she was due to fly out next day. She promised to call in to my work to say goodbye on the way to the airport. She never turned up and I rang and rang and rang until finally she answered. It was a rushed "bye, Mum, gotta go, everything's fine, call you from Berlin" type of call. Her voice was

PARTIES, PILLS & PSYCHOSIS

wobbly and different and distant. I felt quite sick and completely helpless and more so when her Dad told me about the forgotten passport incident.

Three days passed. I had sent messages, made calls, sent emails. Nothing back. I didn't know how else to contact her. I didn't know where she was staying. I kept telling myself she had travelled before, she knew the ropes, she would be OK – the old saying "bad news travels fast" was on constant playback in my mind.

Then came a pathetic two-line email, saying she was OK and, when better sorted, she would write me a "proper email", whatever that was supposed to mean.

I replied, terribly anxious to know what was going on, but was to learn later that she never received my reply. Then came the phone call from the doctor ...

I couldn't speak to Clare for a couple of days because she was so unwell. When I did, I felt quite sick, and – after the initial tears of relief just to hear her voice and know she was alive and safe – it was obvious how garbled she was, incoherent, confused and very scared. She made absolutely no sense at all and I remembered again that this is how it was going to be while she recovered.

Trying to talk to non-English speaking doctors was tricky, but once Adrian liaised with the Australian consulate, which acted as interpreter, the situation improved greatly. Adrian was terrific at making arrangements and sorting things out.

Finding someone to fill in at work for me and booking flights, when initially the doctors said she had to stay in Berlin for three weeks until stabilised, meant the organising was left to the very last minute.

Our GP arranged to have Clare admitted to Alma Street immediately we returned to Perth. The doctors in Berlin said they would give me adequate medication for the trip home. It all seemed to be happening – in a mechanical sort of way, but I was zoned out, sleep-deprived, anxious and frightened and just functioning on autopilot.

Someone suggested I should do some sightseeing in Berlin – hmmm, don't think so.

Adrian had booked me a room in a small hotel about ten minutes' walk from the hospital. Under normal circumstances, I would have said how beautiful the walk was along the river – tree-lined and just gorgeous. But I barely noticed. The hospital was huge and imposing and a very clinical grey in colour – a general hospital with a psychiatric wing. Patients were outside on the lawn area by the river, enjoying the sunshine.

The ward was locked – of course it was. A male nurse answered the bell and let me in. And there was my Clare. We just hugged and hugged and cried and cried and then eventually we let go of each other and she took me to her bed in a shared room. Oh dear, what a mess she was in. Stuff and chaos, mayhem and disorder. I stopped looking because I'd warned myself to expect just that … and I wasn't disappointed.

It's difficult to explain to people what it is like being with someone suffering from psychosis. Maybe it could be assumed that Clare and I would sit quietly together and have a "nice chat" while she filled me in on what had been happening to her. But it's not like that at all.

Lots of words were spoken – but they didn't make sense at all, there weren't any sentences, just staccato words – spoken very quickly and in a low muttering, sometimes completely inaudible, voice.

Clare's eyes couldn't focus on anything and they were vague, distant and bloodshot; her mind couldn't stop wandering, her head would turn, her body constantly moved – she picked things up, put them down, moved something to a place, then moved it somewhere else; she sat down, she stood up, she wandered away and came back again; her thoughts and the subject of her comments changed three times in ten seconds; a fly had more concentration than her at that moment. The paranoia is very strong – she thought people were watching her

PARTIES, PILLS & PSYCHOSIS

and talking about her all the time.

In only a minute or less I was exhausted trying to understand a word she was saying. But I knew it would be like this because "I've been there, done that". So I stopped trying to understand and just listened to her babble, looking at my beautiful daughter reduced to a very undignified, rather pathetic, and very frightened young woman. I just wanted to cry again, but there wasn't much point. She was desperately trying to tell me her story and justify to me (and herself?) the events which had led her to this awful place.

I knew in time, the medication would begin to calm her brain, enabling it to slow down and help her regain some grip on a more normal reality. But for now her reality was a very scary place, out of whack, and making no sense.

I was also really scared that it might not be like that at all. In my reading about psychosis, it was made very clear that in some cases the damage to the brain is too great for full recovery. When I thought about this it made me cry, so I just hardened up and kept that deep within me.

We went down the corridor to meet one of the doctors and nurses. No English in this hospital and my Year 8 German was no help whatsoever. The doctor we had been in contact with for the past two weeks had gone on holiday, but had left instructions and medications. We were allowed to go for a short walk outside and we went along the riverbank, over a bridge and back along the other side to a café. Short walk, but Clare was exhausted. The paranoia was strong – convinced she was being stared at, followed and watched. This was the second time she'd been out in the fresh air for three weeks. She was very intense; trying to tell me what had been going on at the hospital. It was all mumbo jumbo nonsense words.

Back at the hospital, Cory arrived with a few more of Clare's things from the hostel and he filled me in on some of the timeline, but was pretty evasive with the detail. I didn't push it. Clare would spend her last night in the hospital and be discharged into my care on the Sunday.

Hospital dinner over, meds taken, Clare and I cuddled together in her bed until she fell asleep. I said my goodbyes to the night staff and walked back to the hotel.

After a long hot shower, a glass of wine and a phone call home to Adrian, I tried to make sense of Clare's babble and Cory's information. I hadn't slept at all on the flight from Perth, I was completely exhausted and cried myself to sleep.

Next morning Clare was excited to be leaving the hospital and we enjoyed the walk back to the hotel. I had all her meds and instructions. Within five minutes of her being in the room, it looked like hell on earth. Stuff scattered everywhere. (Note to self ¬– chill out, Serena). We planned a ferry ride down the river – a bit of sightseeing to kill time basically – so by lunchtime we were ready to go. Walk, train, walk – sit on the ferry. Gorgeous day, sun was shining. Clare was asleep in less than two minutes, her head resting on my shoulder. So this was my "sightseeing"... See Berlin in One Hour. Except I was too tired to notice much.

We had dinner with Cory that night, just to say goodbye and thank you. From Clare's babble and Cory's chat, I was putting together bits of what had happened. The sequence of events from the party in Perth, taking the drugs that tipped her into a psychotic state, to airport, to Berlin, to hostel, to wandering around the streets of Berlin, alone, in a psychotic daze and various other side-events that finally led to her "arrest by police" and hospitalisation scared me to the very bottom of my soul.

The only conclusion I could come to was that it was only through sheer luck that Clare hadn't been abducted, raped and murdered or got herself completely lost in the city and killed by misadventure or accident.

To this very day I still feel a cold fear gripping me when I think about it. How lucky she is to be alive.

The drugs ensured Clare slept well that night; she was excited to be

PARTIES, PILLS & PSYCHOSIS

going home at last and motivated to get going. We boarded our plane to London at 6 o'clock on Monday morning.

I was even more on edge flying back because I didn't know how Clare was going to be still for 24 hours and more. But it was OK, she slept and listened to her music for most of the journey. We were delayed at every connection and finally landed in Perth late on Tuesday afternoon.

Next day we were due to go to the Alma Street clinic. This is where the fun really started. Now home (and her room trashed in ten minutes), Clare was of the opinion she was OK, all she had to do was slow down and concentrate a little more, she didn't need to go to Alma Street, and "what was all the fuss about?" Oh dear, I had heard this before. The very last people to think they are sick or need help are psychotic patients.

But Adrian and I put our feet down very firmly and on Wednesday morning Clare and I were back at Alma Street triage. This time I was more prepared for a long wait with blanket and pillow. We waited. Clare slept. We waited some more. We were "interviewed" repeatedly and we waited for over four hours before finally going to the ward. Goodness knows why it took so long – Blind Freddie could have seen how desperately unwell she was.

As we entered the lift, I looked across at Clare's vacant, sad face and I nearly burst into tears. It was so awful to be entering this place again. I felt truly sick. Sick with fear and worry and a feeling of complete desperation. Back to the prison-like room, back to some familiar faces of staff members, back to a place of bleakness. The desire to run away from all this was very strong.

Pretty soon I was "shown the door" when a nurse came into Clare's room to do all the admitting procedures. I didn't even make it back to the lift before I was a sobbing mess. I sat in the car crying before I could get it together sufficiently to drive home.

It is long-winded to recount the next three weeks until we transferred

CLARE KENYON

Clare to Perth Clinic, but the first week was so terrible, so unnecessary and entirely the hospital's fault that it should be recorded here.

I knew exactly what Clare's meds were and what strengths they were when we left Berlin and what the doctor had prescribed for the next week at least. There were two different types of medications, Risperidone and Olanzapine. Both were at a significantly higher dosage than her first time, which was quite worrying to me. But Clare was a great deal sicker this time – I didn't need a medical degree to work that one out. Apparently the nursing staff and doctors couldn't work it out and didn't.

The medical report from Berlin was in German. Adrian had done his level best to find someone to translate it – but let's face it, numbers (dosages) are numbers in any language. The English-speaking doctor had been in telephone contact with Alma Street staff, so there shouldn't have been any screw-up.

But there was ... big time.

That evening I rang Clare to see if she was settled. Asking about her meds, she told me she hadn't been given any. Why not? She didn't know. I rang the nurses' station twice that evening and asked to speak to Clare's nurse; she was busy – no one rang me back. I rang Clare again – she still hadn't been given her meds.

Next morning I rang Clare, she had taken her meds – I asked her about the colour and size. The meds had changed. I rang the nursing station again and again but Clare's nurse "was always busy". After work when visiting hours were permitted, I went to see her – as I did every single day.

I was very shocked. She had deteriorated visibly in just a short time. She was fearful, anxious and crying constantly; she made no sense and she was afraid to leave her room. I stayed with her until she went to bed – she wasn't given any meds that night.

I may be a bit of a wallflower dealing with my own issues, but when it comes to protecting my children, I tend to come out with all guns blazing and usually make myself extremely unpopular in the process.

I spoke to Clare's nurse and expressed my concerns. When were we going to see her doctor? Why had the meds changed? Couldn't they see she was worse? What were they doing about it? The nurse wasn't helpful at all. I asked to speak to her doctor – by phone or in person. A whole week went by before we even knew his name!

Adrian was as angry and concerned as I was. He wanted some answers too. Why were the nurses being so cagey? Why couldn't we get answers to our many questions about her drugs, her daily routine, her state of health each day? Where the hell was the doctor?

This "circus" of miscommunication, incompetence, delegation of responsibility and what can only be described as an absence of willingness to do anything, carried on for three days. Clare deteriorated into a truly dreadful place. She was suicidal and I demanded she be placed on suicide watch. Her paranoia and anxiety had reached alarming levels and her muddle-headedness and disassociation with anything approaching reality was really scary. And all this while, we still hadn't spoken to her doctor.

But then it began to get better. I could see her improve, until we were back to the state she was in when we left Berlin – a whole week later.

I knew exactly what had happened. They had found her old file and some smartarse doctor had said – "start her on same as before". No one had bothered to read the discharge notes from Berlin, no one was listening to my incessant haranguing about her medications and her state of health. No one was thinking and no one was caring for Clare. I was beside myself with anger, frustration and fear – all of which Adrian received by the earful when I got home. I was making a thorough nuisance of myself at the nursing station – I could see them diverting their eyes as I approached ... "oh no, here comes that woman again".

Adrian was doing his best to contact the doctor and make an

appointment. He was frustrated at every turn. It was an appalling situation. The "power and authority" these doctors and nurses held over us – her parents – was absolutely dreadful. It was as if we didn't need to know what was going on with Clare's treatment, that it was almost none of our business because Clare was 22 and not a child.

I was to learn that if Clare had signed a release document at the time of her admission stating that we, her parents, could be "part of the care giving team" (oh please, give me a break), then we would have been involved more in her treatment provision and consultations with doctors. All part of the nonsense "privacy laws" compiled by some government bureaucrat sitting in an office, pushing paper at patients' expense. The stupidity of these laws was, of course, Clare – in a psychotic state – couldn't even concentrate or focus long enough to read her name, let alone a legal document. Neither could she understand any instructions from the nurses. So it was over a week before she was even aware of being asked to sign over her permission when I found these documents buried in the mess of her room cupboard. All of this was just like a red rag to a bull for me and I was hell-bent to get her out of this crazy place. "Crazy place?" I shouldn't be calling a hospital a crazy place, don't we all go to hospitals to get well? But that's how Adrian and I felt about the frightening and frustrating situation we found Clare and ourselves in. No-one was listening to us.

Unbeknown to us while Clare was a patient, WA mental health was in the midst of a terrible crisis, which ultimately led to a long, drawn-out government review, many doctors were sacked, and many nurses and doctors left because they were disgusted with it all. Worse still, there were suicides of psychotic and depressed patients, some very young, who had been discharged way too soon with inadequate follow-up care – an appalling situation, and we were in the middle of the mess.

It took another two weeks, during which, admittedly, Clare showed some improvement, before we could get her out of that ghastly place. The problem was no private hospitals would take unstable psychotic patients. At least that was their rule ... until they bumped into me on the end of the phone. I begged, pleaded, and explained, harangued,

PARTIES, PILLS & PSYCHOSIS

argued and begged some more. I was like a dog with a bone – just wouldn't give it up.

In the end, Clare was admitted to Perth Clinic. She was placed under a really caring and "in touch" doctor; he and Clare developed a good rapport and a bond that would continue for another six months. She did various therapies in hospital and when she became an outpatient she did a program of cognitive behaviour therapy.

During the whole time of her hospitalisation and recovery at home her employer at the travel agency had been truly excellent and held her job open until she was ready to resume work. They were caring and concerned about her wellbeing. I think this was a very significant part of her recovery – having a job with purpose, structure, routine and responsibility to get back to so her mind could focus outside of herself. And it would be remiss of me not to mention her group of loyal and caring friends, who stuck with her.

But I felt she needed more support – certainly more than Adrian and I could provide. So I asked one of my customers for help. Michelle is a social worker with a great deal of experience in drug and alcohol-related stuff. I had known her for six years as a customer – she owns a rough collie (which immediately makes her special!). She was delighted to help and we arranged a contra deal with me grooming her lovely collie Lexie. I was pretty sure she and Clare would get on well and they did. Regular weekend chats at a coffee shop became the norm and it was terrific to watch Clare regaining her confidence and slowly putting the pieces of her life back together again.

EMERGING THROUGH THE DARKNESS

"Oh my God, what have I done? All I wanted was a little fun"
The Chemical Brothers – Do It Again

As the weeks dragged by, every day was a struggle. I couldn't put any of the techniques from cognitive behaviour therapy into practice. I hated myself, I was consumed with guilt and I relived Berlin and the trauma I had experienced over and over again. It was the last thing I'd think about before I fell asleep at night and the first thing on my mind when I woke next morning. Everything in the world made me sad, and I would ruminate about my broken life, the mistakes I had made, the failures and the people I had let down. I couldn't believe this had happened to me again – I was right back where I was three years ago. I hadn't learned a thing. I felt like one big loser.

Somehow I would manage to get out of bed, go to work and get through the day. During my lunch break I would often go to the park just to cry, or I would go to the bathroom to let it out. On the train

PARTIES, PILLS & PSYCHOSIS

home, I would openly cry, not caring who saw me – I just couldn't help it. I started smoking more heavily, and drank three or four coffees a day – anything for a high, anything to perk me up, and take away the darkness I felt. I took sick days when it was really bad and I knew I couldn't paint a smile on. One friend at work, Laura, helped me through each day; she always had advice, a smile, a cigarette break and a hug whenever I needed it. She was the main reason I made it through each workday.

I was still on a high dose of medication and it made me lethargic and unmotivated. Also, I gained weight quickly again and never wanted to exercise. It was just another factor that made me miserable, as I had been so slim and beautiful only months before. Now I felt chubby, unattractive and stupid as well as depressed. I dyed my hair dark brown again to reflect the mood I was in; I was back to the miserable, disconnected girl in high school, I wasn't a bubbly, bright, sexy party girl anymore.

Friday August 12, 2011

I feel like I've been stripped down, completely bare, hollow, there's no life in me anymore. I'm at the lowest point I've ever been. Nothing compares to this feeling, not even watching my sister fade away or my brother scream at the world in pain. It's incredible to think about that person I was, so confident, so pretty, so happy, so fun. It feels like a dream it feels like a distant memory. That person I was. Was it so bad? Was it that bad that I can never go back? I never used anything to cover up any depression, I just wanted to have fun. Fun nearly killed me; fun nearly put me in a mental institution for good. It will the next time. I have to be so careful. I'm trying to look at it as a good thing. I'm going to come out much stronger at the other end, if there is ever an end. It's like someone telling you your whole life has been wrong. It hurts so much that I wish I could take the easy way out.

I saw my psychiatrist every two weeks. He prescribed anti-depressants when I eventually admitted I didn't want to be in the world any longer. But I didn't take them; I felt drugs were not the answer for anything anymore, I wanted to get right on my own. And it was a long journey.

We had a six-week and twelve-week follow-up for the cognitive behaviour therapy course at the private hospital. By the six-week session, it was clear I had fallen back down, lower than where I started. At twelve weeks I was still the same and about to go to Bali on a four-day free trip from work, one that Josh and I were planning to go on together. At this follow-up, we learned that Ness had taken her own life. It was an awful, tragic shock. She seemed to be doing well at the previous follow-up. It was so painful to learn, so close to home and she was such a beautiful woman, leaving behind kids and a husband. It reminded me of the pain of depression and mental illness that people suffer in silence; no one can fully understand what they are going through in their minds. It is so scary how people feel so alone and my heart goes out to anyone feeling like that and I wish I could tell them they're not alone and to just reach out.

My friends were all getting on with their lives; they had finished their degrees or courses, they were starting their careers, settling down with partners, buying new cars – which made me feel even worse about myself. I had been to the same school and had got good grades, yet I had been wasting time in a mental hospital. Why was that, I wondered? What was so different? Ah yes, I got into drugs and achieved nothing but learning how to party well. I could open a beer with a lighter; I could roll a perfect cigarette and rack up a perfect line – but who the hell cares? None of it could be regarded as an accomplishment or something that made me employable. Also, I didn't feel like I had reached my potential as a travel agent, and I saw it was just a cop-out from studies yet again.

Monday August 1, 2011

I wish I had never got into drugs. Yes, I've had some great times but I look at my friends who didn't do any of this and how they are getting on with their lives. How they are HAPPY. I think "there's got to be a reason, they know something I don't, they did something I didn't". I always used to think they were squares, close-minded and missing out but really they had their heads screwed on. Ana groaned when I told her I was thinking about changing my hair colour again.

"Oh Clare, you can never be happy," she said.

Easy for you to say, I thought! You have an amazing family, amazing house, lots of friends. Life is perfect for you.

I can't shake this crap feeling. The only time I feel happy is when I'm doing something unhealthy like smoking or rebelling. I hate seeing my friends they just make me feel like shit. I like being at hospital 'cause I connect with people who have problems and I am allowed to be miserable there. Am I destined for a life with problems? This illness has completely pulled me apart, I have no idea how to continue but I'm doing it somehow. Day by day.

I needed a change, a new direction. I couldn't stay in this void, everything reminding me of the failure I was. I would never have the business and the success I dreamed of and I couldn't stand the thought of selling cheap Bali holidays to rude customers for the rest of my life, knowing full well I was smart, had done extremely well at school and could do virtually anything.

My friend had told me simply: "If you can't take care of yourself, how would this business ever work when you have to look after other people?"

And my psychiatrist had said: "You can't start up a business if you are on drugs."

My parents didn't support it any longer as the business would take me to places where drugs were around. And so everything I had worked so damn hard on for a year was lost -- motivation and the belief in myself completely shattered.

Over and over again I would think, I couldn't turn my mind off. If I hadn't done drugs that night, my life would be so different; who knows where that business could have gone, what that meeting in London could have led to, what my boss and I could have worked out for it?

Knowing my determination, though, and how I never give up, I believe I could have seen my plan through to success, which is the part that kills me. I would have stopped partying and focused on the business if I had known there had been a possibility of it happening. But we are all smarter with hindsight. When I was working on it, it felt like my life's purpose and I was so excited I had found what I wanted to do with my life.

If you have ever had a dream, then you would understand how awful it feels to lose it – not from the lack of trying, but through something which was so stupid.

Sunday August 21, 2011

I've never felt lower in my entire life. Like there's no way out, there's no light at the end of the tunnel, nothing to look forward to. All I have is a heavy heart and it hurts so much. I feel like I've lost everything. I lost Josh, I screwed up a holiday, and my dream is over. I lost respect for myself, I've lost confidence, I've lost my will to live because of what has happened. I hate drugs. I hate everything.

My parents desperately wanted me to "reinvent myself" and they said it over and over again. They wanted me to find a new hobby like salsa dancing and make a completely new bunch of friends. The thought just made me more miserable; it meant giving up on dance music and gigs, which is what I loved. They would speak of the scene I was in with disgust, that people in it were all druggies and low lives which I knew not to be true. But how could you explain that to someone who's never experienced it? They were so afraid I would get back into it a third time and so they didn't want me to go there ever again. And I stayed away, despite my misery. When the people I loved didn't accept me for who I was anymore, I couldn't accept myself either. My IPod really only had house music, breakbeat and drum n bass on it and I almost hated listening to it, so I dug up old albums and would listen to sad songs like Take You Away by Angus and Julia Stone on the bus, tears just streaming down my face, feeling so devastatingly lonely.

PARTIES, PILLS & PSYCHOSIS

Thursday September 1, 2011

Identity. What does that even mean anymore? All I know is the past, that fun person I used to be. I miss me. Now I just don't know. I miss Josh so much, I know he wasn't the right guy for me but is that just because I've been listening to psychologists and parents for two months solid? Can you ever go back? I don't know how to live anymore. I'm just going day by day and eventually it will work itself out, right? I feel like I need to be away from people for a really long time.

Dad tried to console me as often as he could. He would sit with me and hold my hand, talking about his life, how one decision led to another decision, which led to another decision. I knew he was trying to explain that life is a journey and that different things lead to things you cannot plan for. I knew he was trying to make me realise what I was going through now was not forever and one day this would all be behind me. I knew he wanted me to think there was a light at the end of the tunnel. I knew he was trying so hard to make me smile and make me understand it was OK and he wasn't angry with me anymore. But I just kept on crying.

Saturday October 5, 2011

The doc started me on anti-depressants today. I probably should start taking them. Every day when I get off at the train station I imagine throwing myself off over the bridge to the freeway. Then I wouldn't have to feel like this anymore.

Saturday October 12, 2011

I'm not beautiful or confident, I don't have any skills, I'm not good at anything. I make terrible decisions and I let guys treat me like crap. The one good promising thing I had in my life I ruined. Josh ruined it. He's such a prick. How did I get involved with a guy like that? Where did I go wrong? I hate guys; all they do is hurt you. I hate Josh for ruining my life. Who the hell has meow meow at a party?

CLARE KENYON

Friday October 25, 2011

I feel barely human these days. I can't make conversation with people I meet, I sit and listen and don't say a word. I'm so introverted now. I can't feel a thing except unhappiness. I feel numb. I can't stop feeling sorry for myself. I hate it, I hate me, I wish I was loud and beautiful and confident like every other girl out there. I wish I could decide what to do with my life. I wish I could figure out what I want and what makes me happy.

I went through every emotion – anger, blame, guilt, hatred. After a while, I was so unhappy Mum started to break down because she didn't know how to help me anymore. Every Saturday, after I forced myself out of bed, I would go and see her at her dog grooming salon. But instead of it being a nice visit, I would just start bawling. We would sit out the back and she would just hold me. And then Mum would cry with me. I think that broke my heart even more, knowing I was still causing her so much pain when all I ever wanted was for my parents to be happy.

Mum enlisted the help of one of her friends – a social worker named Michelle. I met with her every two weeks for coffee and got it all out. It was such a relief to not dump it on Mum anymore. Michelle really got me and understood everything about giving up drugs and what that meant, because it wasn't just a hobby, it was part of my identity and the life I had been living for so many years. I was a party animal and that was my world. So I had no idea who I was anymore or who I could be. Michelle was the most incredible support and became a good friend. She also became my go-to for advice with virtually everything that happened to me over the next year of my life.

Firstly, I wanted to pay my parents back and get the debt out of the way. Mental illness is not covered by travel insurance, so the flights they had to buy for Mum to get to Berlin, plus the hospital bills came to around $10,000 - money I certainly didn't have, nor my family, so we borrowed it from Grandma.

As money, or lack thereof, has been such a massive issue for my family, this debt contributed to my feeling dreadful and not being able

PARTIES, PILLS & PSYCHOSIS

to just "get over" what happened – especially since, only a couple of months earlier, I believed I would own a business one day that would make our family disgustingly rich and my parents would finally be able to live apart and get on with their lives. I thought that perhaps I could get a job in the mines and pay it back quickly. I tried for jobs and contacted people who were in the industry but nothing eventuated, plus my parents kept trying to tell me it was OK and I could pay it back one day.

I thought seriously about moving to the East Coast to spend time with my sister Natalie, who was about to have her first baby. I thought seriously about getting a second job and working nights to save up and move to Canada to travel and work on the ski fields. Dad, Emma, Natalie and I flew to the Gold Coast for another entrepreneur seminar to see if that would ignite something within me.

But when it came down to it, I wanted an education now and I wanted to go back to university to finish my degree. I had no idea what to study and wanted desperately to get it right this time. I thought seriously about doing a health degree and moving away to complete the course ... running away? But I knew in my heart I needed to stick it out at home.

At my parents' suggestion, I went to a psychologist who specialised in career profiling and did a few tests with him. The results indicated my best options were either social work or journalism. I loved to write so I picked the latter, applied and was accepted two days later.

The major drama during my recovery was with Josh. We had broken up before I started Cognitive Behaviour Therapy, but he promised he would contact me all the time and we would remain friends. I didn't hear from him, which didn't surprise me, but I started to worry because I had lent him $1500 for his apartment bond before I went to Europe and he promised he would pay it back. After two months of phone calls and texts it was clear he wasn't going to. Dad became angry and took charge. He drafted up a letter which he made Josh sign. It said something along the lines of "I, Josh, owe this money to Clare and will pay it back by this date, or if I don't, I acknowledge that they will take legal action against me".

Of course he didn't pay it back in time, so we filed a lawsuit. He didn't do anything after the first set of court documents were sent to him, so the next stage was completing a means enquiry, which took months to sort out.

Thursday November 17, 2011

I caught up with Josh tonight. Dad got him to sign a letter saying he owed me this money. Then we sat and chatted for a while. It was so good to catch up with him, see his gorgeous face and laugh with him again. I do miss him but I think I just miss having someone. He gave me this enormous hug at the end and kissed me and it felt like someone was pulling at my heart. All I wanted was to stay in that moment. And then I was all flustered when we broke apart. He's hit rock bottom too, he's completely broke and has lost his job. I really know now he's not the right guy, not boyfriend material but just someone fun, more like a fantasy. And I liked who I was with him. I think that's more the point. Cute, sexy, fun party girl Clarey. Not recovering mentally ill girl.

A couple of months down the track a girl contacted me on Facebook. Out of the blue she wrote: "I don't know if you know me but I was the other girl while you were seeing Josh."

So all of a sudden I found out he had been cheating on me. She also told me he had herpes. I went and got myself checked and by some miracle I was OK. She also told me he had borrowed money from her and she was also trying to get it back. Then weeks later I found out he had been in jail.

So after months of no contact, I called him and questioned him. Not surprisingly, he denied everything. I couldn't believe he was cheating on me when I was sick, in hospital.

However, he offered no apology. And I asked him why the hell he didn't tell me he had herpes, but again he answered with denial and

PARTIES, PILLS & PSYCHOSIS

lame excuses.

Perhaps this is what the endless drug use did to him, I thought; led him to treat people without care or respect. Had I also become like this, I wondered?

I hung up eventually and pushed what he did out of my mind. I was happy he was out of my life; he really was not a good person and am forever grateful to Dad for taking charge of that aspect of my life when I was so confused back in hospital.

Tuesday November 8, 2011

"You need to completely reinvent yourself," Mum yelled at me. *"Over my dead body will your father and I let you go back to the lifestyle that has threatened your life"*...

Those words echo over and over in my head. This was my identity, how I got through life, how I survived for the past three years. How can I find anything else that will make me that happy but keep me healthy?

Saturday December 3, 2011

This used to be my city, where I roamed free, where I dressed up in my gorgeous heels or kicks and danced and laughed until I couldn't any longer. It was mine. My happiness. Now I sit back and look at those girls and feel like an outcast, far from that girl I once knew and the thought constantly turns over in my head, if I hadn't got into drugs maybe I wouldn't be in this position. Depressed, chubby, in debt. My nights were the centre of my world, now that world is no longer. I remember the days when nothing scared me, I would walk up to anyone, say anything, do anything, fearless, unstoppable, confident. I was on top of the world and nothing could bring me down. But as it turned out I crumbled, my mind gave way. I abused the precious thing that we are given and it hurt me back. Stopped me from getting the things I wanted in life. I went too hard and ruined the things I loved most. Now all I have is a heavy heart. It hurts so much. I don't look at myself in the mirror anymore, I don't like what I see. There's a stranger staring back at me. It's never the same anymore when I go out, I don't feel it like I used to. I guess that's the high drugs give you.

You just assume one day you will be happy again, but what if you never do and you just live with this constant pain. Maybe I've been unhappy my whole life and I've never realised it.

Thursday December 22, 2011

This can't be my life, my job. I don't want this to be all there is. I want something bigger, greater, more passionate. I want to be excited and empowered. I want to move forward but I'm hopelessly stuck here.

Sunday January 1, 2012

I brought the New Year in with tears streaming down my face while I lay in bed at Sarah's house. I am so scared, unhappy, miserable and confused and I don't know what to do about it. I don't want this year to start; I just wish time would stand still for me but it moves so quickly. I am still not over what happened. I think about it all the time. When I'm with my friends I feel lonely, insecure and shy. I'm about to turn 23 soon, I don't feel grown up or mature. I don't feel like I've accomplished anything. Why is life only about getting a good job so you can earn money and live? It seems so simple and pointless, like there's nothing to it. Nothing exciting, passionate, dangerous. My parents tell me over and over again I have to change. I don't know how to do it. Abandon the only thing that made me happy? But it isn't safe for me. But anything's got to be better than feeling as low as this. I wish my head would stop hurting. It feels like someone is constantly squeezing it. And my eyes hurt from endless tears. My world is dark and nothing ever makes me smile.

Not even the festival season made me feel better this time around. I was so horribly low and I never knew if I would ever stop feeling this way. Parklife was difficult because Josh and I always used to talk about

PARTIES, PILLS & PSYCHOSIS

the pre and after-party we'd have for it as his apartment was right near the venue. So I knew I'd be missing out – the asshole even texted me on the day just to dig it in a bit. I ignored him and was glad to go with Lucy and her boyfriend who understood the place I was in.

It was hard to start going to gigs again as the Perth electronic dance music scene had a clique of regulars and I was bound to bump into someone I knew. I felt like everyone knew what had happened to me, because of my paranoia in Berlin when I went on Facebook. The massiveness of my psychotic episode was that I thought the whole world knew what was happening and was laughing at me and although I didn't think those thoughts anymore, it shattered my confidence to be out in public. I was so embarrassed, I wasn't sure who I'd see out and have to talk to, I hadn't fully accepted this had happened to me anyway. I didn't even know how to go out sober.

I don't think I went back to Barrick until around January 2012, about six months later when I decided to meet up with Jayden again. But it was all in my head and the people I spoke to were generally just worried for me.

I hadn't really caught up with Jayden for a long time, but he knew what had happened to me. I mention him now because he really has contributed to my getting better in so many ways. Jayden is a friend who I go out shuffling with and we have become very close. He has probably been one of the best influences in my life. In a way, he understands me better than anyone because he has been in the drug scene himself. But now he chooses to go out and party sober and make health his first priority, while still enjoying the dance music scene. He is a role model for me and I learned I could have an absolute blast without drugs. He has taught me many things about safe, natural energy alternatives, including certain foods. He and two other friends I became closer with over this time, Mace and Cassy, made it easier for me. I realised I didn't have to do this on my own. I realised there were people out there in the scene that party sober and have a good time.

My 23rd birthday came around in February 2012; my friends had all come over for drinks and the regular Barrick night. I made a little speech thanking them for their support over the past six months. They had helped me through it, encouraged me, and reminded me who I was and the Clare without drugs is better than Clare with them and they would always love me. I was grateful Sarah had forgiven me.

Friends like Zoe and Joe would take me out for beers and get me out of my head. They would remind me that shit just happens and would tell me to "just stop thinking". My sister Charlotte, who had battled depression, is a strong person I look up to, and a reminder there's always a light at the end of the tunnel.

And then my parents ... they are incredible people for sticking by me after everything I put them through. There are stories of families kicking their kids out – some being the patients I met in hospital. I am eternally grateful they stayed by my side.

I got off my medication in February. I hated the way it made me feel and I knew all the psychotic thoughts had gone and my mind had recovered. I stopped seeing my psychiatrist and once I made the decision about university and to go backpacking again, I started to feel better. I started to move on.

Sunday April 1, 2012

I haven't written for a long time. I guess that's because I am finally happy. It took a while but I'm there. I love my friends I couldn't have done it without them. People like Jayden have got me through it. He understands me, encourages me to party sober and understands my happy place and that I can't let it all go. I've decided on journalism, I love to write, I can't believe I didn't think of it earlier. I'm going to Asia to backpack on my own and I have even met a guy who's taken an interest in me. I feel strong again, fun, bright and I can joke again, party and muck around without feeling the guilt. I think I've started to forgive myself. Happiness is found. It's the music that brought me back and accepting that that part of me will never change.

FOUR YEARS ON

"Paradise ... now I know it's not some place you can look for. Because it's not somewhere you can go. It's how you feel for a moment in your life when you feel a part of something. And if you find that moment ... it lasts forever."
Richard – The Beach

NYE 2013/14 Las Vegas

Graduation day February 2015

CLARE KENYON

Monday June 6, 2014

New diary. New words. What will become of this one I wonder? It feels so good to close the last chapter and move on. Ironic that I am heading back to Berlin again? I'm not so sure, I know it's the writer within me that sees it that way. And like Jason said I need to see it in a positive way, instead of being nervous and scared. I am going to see Charlotte after all. There's nothing to be afraid of now. Only new memories, new dreams, new goals, new words, descriptions, sentences and a fascination with something. A new story is out there for me to find.

When I went back to Berlin in 2014 to visit my sister who was living in Germany, I looked at it as a way to put it all behind me, once and for all. Sometimes I didn't believe it to be real, it still seemed so far-fetched at times that it had happened at all. But I went back to the hospital, I stood in front of that place again and realised how far I had come because of it. The experience has shaped me into the woman I am today. And in a small, weird way I am grateful.

The years of turmoil, confusion and sadness have led me along a path to confidence, success and happiness. Even as the illness drained all that was left of me, I was given a chance to restart, to find strength, build myself up and assess what I actually hold true and dear. A day does not go by when I don't remember how lucky I am to have made it through at all.

After about a year the dark cloud hanging over me began to lift, and I sealed my new-found happiness with a two-month holiday in South-East Asia in 2012, feeling like the adventurer once more with a backpack on, a passport in hand and no set plan. It made me feel fearless again, reinvigorated, like I was ready to take on the world. I fell back in love with life – with its simplicity and its hardship; and with its beauty, adventure and uncertainty. I got a third tattoo while I was away, one from The Beach movie, to remind myself that I had found paradise within and that the journey of life was truly beautiful, no matter what happened.

When I returned home university started and while I sat in my first

PARTIES, PILLS & PSYCHOSIS

unit of journalism, a spark lit up inside me. My interest in writing, and my curious and inquiring mind could be used on something worthwhile. There was a career for me, and like any idealistic student journalist, I thought my stories could help make a change in the world.

At this time I was happily single, strong and independent, enjoying my new outlook on life. Dating bad boy after bad boy taught me a lot, but it had brought me down. My self-esteem had been so low I went for these bad boy party types and I made unnatural connections through drugs, which is probably why they all broke down. Because my life had been consumed with boyfriends I had never developed a notion of who I was, and I developed self-destructive habits. But now I was confident enough to be on my own, I no longer needed a man to prop me up and I finally got to a place where I knew I deserved someone who would treat me well.

It was then that I met a blond American boy whose blue eyes made me weak. I knew as soon as I met him he would turn my world upside down. I had been hesitant to give my number out to anyone because my sense of self-worth was the highest it had ever been and I was not going to give my heart to just anybody again. But this time felt different to the others; this was why I went through the broken hearts, tears and bullshit. Now I loved myself and I was comfortable in my own skin to be exactly myself. And he loved me for it. It has since developed into a wonderful relationship and he is the man I want to spend the rest of my life with.

Despite the cruel hands that were dealt to my parents over and over again, they were getting by. My Mum's business, which started out as a little mobile dog grooming round, developed twelve years later into a fantastic proper salon. She also owned a second pet food business for a while and has become very passionate about animal welfare. Due to a cancer scare, Mum had to slow the businesses down and she looked to greener pastures. And as the strong, smart, hard-working woman that I love, she started on a new venture. Mum and I are incredibly close now, I look on her as a best friend and someone I can share everything with.

CLARE KENYON

My sister has been healthy and happy for many years now. She was studying at the WA Academy of Performing Arts for a while before she deferred and moved to Germany with her boyfriend. After more than a year, she came home fluent in German, with a new zest for life.

My brother is the happiest he has ever been. He has matured and is doing well in his career as a metal fabricator. Chris recently married his highschool girlfriend and they bought a home together back in 2010. I was a bridesmaid at his wedding and it was one of the most special days of my life. My Dad retired as a journalist but continues to play piano for ballet classes at schools and dance studios. I have a good relationship with him, we understand each other and I love that I know him now and he is an active person in my life.

I realise after all this how he puts his family above everything else, and has tried so hard, especially in recent times, to make our family work. He has the sweetest heart and a beautiful, intelligent, deep mind which I hope I am lucky enough to have inherited. His support throughout everything with Josh and how he was so protective of me made me realise how much he loves me and I am proud to call him my Dad. What I saw of my Mum and Dad through the eyes of a fourteen-year-old way back then doesn't do justice to what they were both going through. But that is part of the naivety and innocence of childhood.

After everything was out in the open, my relationship with my parents improved greatly, and we could all move on. I know they were relieved when I got stuck into university and found an interest outside of the party scene. After a while they stopped worrying when I went out to drum and bass gigs with Jayden because they knew I was no longer taking drugs. Somehow I managed to convince them I could have fun without substances and those nights were still my happy time, my chance to dance and escape and laugh. I found myself at festivals and gigs watching on as ravers mucked around with their friends like I used to, with that invincible attitude that came across as arrogance. I know that's how I used to act. I remembered how the higher and more fucked up you got drinking and taking drugs, the more hardcore, more funny or 'cooler' you became within your group of mates. Now I just shake my head at the stupidity of it all. I had built up this ego

PARTIES, PILLS & PSYCHOSIS

on a chemical high, thinking I knew something nobody else did but it was only when I stepped away did I realise it meant nothing. I was somebody in a nightclub, but I was nothing in real life. The cockiness I used to feel disappeared almost instantly after Berlin. Nothing I had experienced was cool.

I was lucky to have made a group of friends who were no longer interested in getting drunk or getting high but still enjoyed the music I liked. They had all been part of the drug scene once, but they had moved on from it and not without their own bad experiences. Having that positive influence around me made it a lot easier to move on as well. Once I started talking more about what had happened to me, I realised that it was not uncommon for people, and yet we all used to parade around as if everything was ok. Party people tended to turn a blind eye to the dark side of drugs until it was too late.

Unfortunately, my friendships with Lucy and Sarah crumbled as I spoke to them about writing this book. They and my other high school friends, who I became so close to again during my recovery, distanced themselves from me and would not support me in this journey. Although it was extremely hurtful at the time, I've tried to understand their reasoning and not let it ruin any more friendships. But it will never be the same.

Learning to let go was a big lesson for me, as I just wanted everything to stay the same for a while. Friendships can be lost naturally or on purpose but it doesn't take away from how important they were at a certain time. My high school group will always have a special place in my heart, no matter what has come to pass. Lucy, Sarah and the rest of the cuzzies taught me a lot about myself and they were a part of my life for a reason.

Since we began high school together, my friendship with Cara has been tried and tested, and yet she has always stuck by me. I consider myself extremely lucky to have her constant support, despite our differences. Cory saved my life and I'll never forget it and even as he continues to travel the world, he will always be someone I hold very dear.

CLARE KENYON

In 2015, after two and a half years at university, I walked proudly on stage to receive my Bachelor's Degree with my parents, brother, sister and partner watching on. It had been a busy, stressful, exciting and inspiring time that had opened me up to new people, teachers and opportunities. My final year's work also saw me selected as a finalist in the 2015 WA Media Awards. As graduation loomed, so did the apprehension about gaining employment at a time when uncertainty in the media is rampant, but I was lucky enough to be noticed during my internship at Western Australia's daily newspaper and offered a job on a highly regarded regional newspaper where many great Australian journalists also started out.

And so my writing career started, the forgotten dream of a young girl. I look back now and wonder what took me off track so early on, how I strayed from the path that I am on now. Can I put it down to a troubled teenage life, a broken family, or merely my curiosity and rebellious nature? What draws a person into the drug scene? I will never forget that very first time at the Future Music Festival, when Liam looked over knowingly at my smiling face and said: "fuckin' good fun, isn't it?" Was it really that simple for me? A desire to have some fun and a bit of peer pressure which led me to become so sick?

Everyone's story is different; there are many reasons why some people will get into it, and others won't. Why was I affected by peer pressure more than others? Why wasn't I scared off by media stories about teenagers dying, like my high school girlfriends were? All my life I was searching for something but never sure of what it was. I wanted to escape something, but always returned back to my home. Was it inevitable for me to chase all possible experiences when some would turn out as bad as this did?

I don't want to act like the past few years have been easy and drugs have never resurfaced in my life again. The more I wanted it to vanish from my life completely, the more I realised how normal it is now for many people – teenagers, twenty-somethings, young professionals, white collar workers, parents, couples, well adjusted, smart people. There would be no escape for me. Also, it was virtually impossible to stop drinking alcohol, although I don't drink like I used to. It's a reflection of the culture we live in, everything is celebrated with alcohol. Our culture sends the message that if we want to have a good time we need to drink, it is the way young people now operate. There is a huge amount of peer pressure to drink in our society and by choosing not to, you are automatically cast as the odd one out instead of being celebrated for taking the healthier road.

Similarly, there is a culture around drugs that cannot be disregarded. Mainstream and underground artists endorse it in music like it is something cool to do and it's celebrated in popular movies, so no wonder people can fall into it so easily. Music festivals have become a drug playground and are growing in popularity, as is the Electronic Dance Music scene which undeniably has a large drug culture attached to it. With weed becoming legal in the United States, it automatically sends the message that it is acceptable now. All these things are making it more normal and sometimes hard to say no when a friend offers something to you.

So in the end, for me, it came down to choosing to live a healthier life, rather than something happening which forced me to change. It was empowering to realise what had happened wasn't making me change into someone who was less likely to throw caution to the wind and just get wasted like everyone else. Now I actually wanted to live a different, healthier lifestyle and knowing that gave me the confidence to not get into it again. I was now in control of my life and the choices I made because I respected my body, my brain and my health. I got a kick out of it, just like drugs had done for me years ago, but now I got a kick out of feeling free to be me without anything extra.

I had given chemicals the flick and learned the joy of feeling healthy highs. I stopped having boozy nights which resulted in me wasting the next day feeling awful, but I still was able to go out, have fun and dance with my friends because I was literally high off being alive. I stopped eating bad food that made me feel sluggish and fat and instead I got high on good food, endorphins and fell in love with exercising. I was healthier than I had ever been in my life – mind body and soul healthy – and this gave me a sense of real happiness I never thought was possible, and that feeling would last my entire life, not just one night.

CLARE KENYON

I didn't realise what a self-indulgent, self-destructive life I was living until I was on the outside looking in. I used to just accept the comedowns, the after-anxiety, the overthinking as being part of it, but now I would never voluntarily put my body through that again. Sometimes it would take all week to feel 'normal' again after a big weekend. I hated those nights when I'd come home, still feeling wired, and just stare at the wall waiting for sleep to come over me. I used to blow $200, $300 on a night that I would have no memory of the next day, and instead have to deal with a terrible hangover. What was the point? Four weekends of that is a plane ticket to Europe.

When I got to a good place, my mind started to tick over about the next generation of party people. That sense of invincibility and disregard for what we put into our bodies and the lack of thought, caution and consequence for any action. It embodies that time in our life, when we are young and carefree, we have absolutely no idea what seemingly small decisions can lead to, but we don't care. We live for the moment, for the night. It's easier to not think about the consequences or the irreparable damage drugs can do because having fun with our mates is the priority.

We choose to take risks maybe because we see our best friends doing it, and they are fine, so why not, right? The dilemma seems to be that the majority generally get away with it and so there is a disassociation with health warnings or advice. But we don't think about our future self or how we will end up when we're at a party, gearing up for a big night with friends. I wish everyone who did drugs, or was about to try them, could spend a week in a psychiatric ward and see what happens when you lose control of your mental health. Watch the brain dead patients, the men who can't dress themselves, the women who mumble to themselves, and then count the endless numbers of drug-induced psychotic people who get admitted every weekend.

Stand there and feel what it's like to be in that ward, imagine for a second it is your life. It would wake you up, that's for sure; and it would make you realise how important your health, your brain and your body are, and how serious a risk you take every time you party hard. Because right now you might be fine, but you don't know what

PARTIES, PILLS & PSYCHOSIS

could happen after a couple of months or years of partying.

It's innately human to want to belong and feel accepted by people around you. Regardless of your choice of lifestyle everyone will feel peer pressure at some stage. When it comes down to it, you're a product of your environment, so if you want to live a certain way you need to surround yourself with certain people. When you're young it's even harder; you're just finding your way in the world and you might not have the confidence to stand on your own two feet. I wish I could tell that unhappy 16-year-old-girl, confused about where she fit into the world, it would not always be like that.

No one would ever egg me on and say "come on, Clare, have another bong, do another line". In the beginning it was more the pressure I put on myself to be a part of the group that I wanted to hang out with. Perhaps there was a silent expectation from other people as well and once I was a part of it, it was just a given that's what I did. I was very young, wanting to feel like I belonged somewhere and was attracted to the fun of it all. And so a path into the drug scene was formed.

Adolescence is the experimenting age where boundaries and limits are tested. Unfortunately, it is also the worst time to do it as your brain is still developing and you have little knowledge about drugs or yourself. It is undisputed now the effects on your brain from drug use from a young age can stay with you for the rest of your life and I feel certain I became so unwell because I started smoking at a young age. After researching it, I'm also sure it is why I have a terrible memory now. The likelihood of addiction and illness climbs dramatically higher, the earlier you try something. Adolescence is also a time when you can so easily get on the wrong path and so it is safer to avoid it at all costs until there is a time in your life when you know all the facts and are completely conscious of the choice you are making.

The line is too blurry between those who will get away with it and those who won't. You don't know if it will be the 1st pill, or the 51st pill, 4th bong or the 400th bong that sends you over the edge, so why play Russian roulette with your life, just for one fun night. Think about the hundreds, thousands, millions that take the chance and do not get away with it. Those left on the sidewalk or in and out of hospital wards all their life. Those kept below the surface, battling addictions, mental illnesses or who get into crime to feed a habit. They come out time and time again to tell their story, like I have. But they weren't always that person. They started out in the world just like me and you.

You don't know if you'll be the one that gets paranoid, or gets hungry for more. As a teenager you would never think a harmless smoke with friends would lead you into a life of addiction, crime or illness. When you see the damage drugs can do first hand and the pain it brings to families, it is just not worth it.

Which brings me to my last thought.

How will I teach my daughter when I send her off to high school, what will I say to her? Will she understand if I sit her down and tell her about psychosis, addiction, the people I met in hospital? Will it be enough to scare her off a lifetime of gambles that will undoubtedly come before her? Will she fall into the category of curiosity...wanting to know how it felt, why they called it ecstasy, what the funny stoner movies were all about. Will she fall into the rebellious category and decide to take the risk because her mother said she shouldn't? If she didn't try a thing will she wonder if she was missing out on something?

Sometimes it seems hard to know what the answers are when you consider that four states in the USA have now legalized recreational weed and the YES campaign is gearing up throughout the rest of the country. Meanwhile, the UK and Australia still have the highest numbers of recreational drug users; teenagers continue to lose their lives at dance festivals or to addiction; the ice epidemic is wreaking havoc throughout homes worldwide, hospitals continue to battle psychosis on a daily basis; treatment, mental health and rehab facilities are crying out for more investment …. In the light of all this the War on Drugs looks more and more like an epic failure. And as young people, medical professionals, politicians and law enforcers appear so divided on how to deal with it, I wonder if there is an answer at all. But we must never lose hope.

PARTIES, PILLS & PSYCHOSIS

My hope is that I can teach my children how important their mental health is and why they must take care of it in every possible way in everything they do. I hope I can equip them at a young age with knowledge and facts about drug use, health effects and mental health illnesses, so they can make informed decisions through an honest and open conversation. I hope I can send them out into the world knowing they can trust me and they can tell me anything at all, and that my story shows how important it is to ask for help when they need it.

I hope I am their go-to person when someone breaks their heart or fills it with joy. I hope they won't abuse my trust like I did to my own mother and instead realise I am on their side. I hope I can teach them life is exactly what they make it and I can show them how to be resilient and strong like my family is. I hope I can help them to figure out what the journey of life is really all about, and what true happiness feels like.

I hope what I went through will be a lesson for my children, a lesson for you, to always take care of your mental health, to respect the very precious thing that is uniquely yours. And to take heed of this warning. It is not worth the risk to your life, your brain and your body. Instead, use your time in the world to explore, to learn and to love.

Life is a very precious journey, and you only get one, so keep searching to find your healthy high.

FINAL NOTE FROM MUM

by Serena Kenyon

It was a throwaway line from her doctor that did it ..."write your story down, Clare, it is terrific therapy". Clare took up the suggestion and wrote her story...in all its ugliness. Warts and all, as they say. In so doing, Clare matured as a person. The process changed her attitude, her purpose and her emotions. What started out as, "Doctor says I should write this, Mum, because he believes it will be good for me" became "Maybe if I write this it will help other young people who may be going off the rails, like I did".

Clare has done a lot of growing up over these past five years. She reached rock bottom and has climbed back up the hill again. Her father and I are very proud of her. Having our own stumblings as parents and life's dirty laundry laid out bare for all to read hasn't been much fun – but full marks to Clare for having the courage to tell all. Although it's a confronting read for us, we didn't shy away from her wanting to do this. Instead, we were full of encouragement as she progressed with it.

I want to say I feel entitled to fiercely defend Clare's desire to write this book and her intentions for the potential use of the information it contains, against what can only be described as an ignorant and unkind

PARTIES, PILLS & PSYCHOSIS

backlash from a few of her "friends". I have watched Clare cope with all the rejection and hurt. She is a resilient young woman now on the brink of a promising journalistic career and I am so very proud of her.

This book may never see the light of day as a published product, but I hope it does. I also hope – as does Clare – it may act as a red light warning to young people heading down the drug road and an "aide-memoire" for the Mums and Dads out there.

AFTERWORD

"Parties, Pills and Psychosis" is a frank, honest account of Clare Kenyon's journey through what was for her a tumultuous adolescence and young adulthood. Through this book, Clare gives us the privilege of examining her life, and one doesn't get much more personal than excerpts from a diary. Along the way, I gleaned a number of important messages.

To those in their teens and twenties, Clare's story tells us that drugs don't fix the turmoil. Certainly, she makes no secret of how good it feels when using, but at the end of it she sees the truth that substances don't lead to happiness, don't lead to contentment, and don't lead to peace with oneself. If you are young and to read this book, I think you will empathise with what Clare describes, and hopefully it can steer you away from some of the mistakes that she feels she made in her time.

For parents there are a number of important messages. First of all, drugs feel good and your kids know it. Educate yourself about them. You can't demonise them, especially when they provide such elation, such connection with others and such a sense of belonging, as Clare describes. It's important to acknowledge this but also be there for your kids when the inevitable downsides you tell them about come to pass. Serena, Clare's mum, shares the agony of a parent seeing the suffering that drugs bring. Maybe, she could have been more aware, maybe she could have been more nosey, maybe she could have kept enquiring despite the resistance, but I can only admire that she managed to do the one thing that is really important for a parent in this circumstance – she kept the relationship going, and Clare knew

PARTIES, PILLS & PSYCHOSIS

that mum cared and would be there when she was ready. As I see it, parents participate in giving their children life but it's their life and they need to live it. With this come the choices that the kids make, and of course it's important to teach, to lead, to enquire, to correct, and at the same time to dish out whatever consequences might be relevant - but it has to be tempered with knowing that your kids (and all people) only change when they are uncomfortable, whatever perils parents might see.

For mental health care professionals, Clare's message is to be consistent, to be understanding, to be faithful, to try and "connect", to try to "educate", but in the end, people will change when they are ready. Every once in a while a story like Clare's will emerge, and that makes all the care extra-ordinarily worthwhile.

I wish there was a message that would change society. I wish there was something that Clare could say that would light the way for us as a community. I wish there were words that I could string together to make it different. In the end, we all have to take responsibility for our own choices and actions, and Clare has done this, to her great credit. For those already starting to experience the consequences, the problems, the discomfort that drugs lead to, Clare's story can be an encouragement that life can be different, that there is a way. Keep on searching.

Dr. C. Nick De Felice, M.B.B.S., F.R.A.N.Z.C.P

ABOUT THE AUTHOR

Clare Kenyon is 27 and currently living in Waco, Texas, with her fiancé, Jason. Before moving to America in 2016, she was working in regional WA at a daily newspaper reporting on health, the courts, business and Aboriginal affairs. You can catch up with Clare on her blog www.clarekenyon.net.

REFERENCES

1. Bursary - 50% off school fees based on grades.
2. Anorexia Nervosa - eating disorder characterised by irrational fear of gaining weight and immoderate food restriction.
3. Bong - water bottle through which you smoke marijuana.
4. Sessions/sesh - when people get together to smoke marijuana.
5. Cannies - a tin can through which you smoke marijuana.
6. Buckets - a method of smoking marijuana through a bigger bong/bucket giving you a greater effect.
7. UDL - a popular "alcho-pop" drink.
8. Dexies - dexamphetime. Prescription medication for ADD kids. Often used as a party drug or study aid.
9. Ecstacy - a pill containing Methylenedioxy-n-methylampethamine (MDMA).
10. Munchies - hunger effect from getting stoned and slang term for food.
11. Baggie - a small plastic bag of marijuana/or other drugs.
12. Cone - metallic cone used in a bong. Slang expression for smoking marijuana.
13. Kicks - slang for shoes, primarily sneakers.
14. Pingerz - slang for ecstasy.
15. Gurning - the muscle tension in the face that usually ends up with the jaw and tongue rolling and teeth grinding as a result of amphetamine use.
16. Melbourne Shuffle - a rave and club scene dance originating in Melbourne in the 80s.
17. Biccies - slang for ecstasy.
18. Jagerbombs - a drink combining a shot of Jager with Red Bull energy drink.
19. R2D2 - A fluoro analog of amphetamine, 4-Fluoroamphetamineproduces stimulant and possibly empathogenic or psychoactive effects.

CLARE KENYON

www.ingramcontent.com/pod-product-compliance
Lightning Source LLC
Chambersburg PA
CBHW070605300426
44113CB00010B/1413